MW01089242

Red Grosse
Oktheumpka
11-29-17

Skeeters and Hogs and Mules, Oh My!

Red Fussell

Sandy Oard Kruse
Ruth McIntyre Williams

Published 2017
Barefoot Publications
Okahumpka, Florida

Transcribed and edited by Sandy Oard Kruse
Edited and book design by Ruth McIntyre Williams

The cover artist, Pamela Jaworski, was born and raised south of Chicago. She won a scholarship to the Art Institute of Chicago and the Chicago Academy of Fine Arts, attended the University of Missouri and sold her first painting at the age of 18. After nearly twenty years of raising three children and running a commercial art company with her husband in New England and Orlando, Pamela decided to get back into painting full-time.

In the past ten years collectors throughout the world have enjoyed Pamela's work. Her work is exhibited in a number of galleries throughout the US and also with Howard Alan Events.

"I hope you enjoy my work. I give thanks to God for His beautiful creation and the opportunity He has given me to bring these inspirational moments into my work."

Pamela Jaworski
jawo4106@att.net

List of Tales

Skeeters and Hogs and Mules, Oh, My!

This is a work of truth and fiction. All the character names are friends of the author and of his imagination in and around Okahumpka, Florida. The book was written to show the reader just how the poor entertained themselves and just how creative they could be. All the names of the places are true, but as far as the story goes, believe the parts you want to.

Skeeters and Hogs and Mules, Oh My!

Photo Note: All photographers who contributed to this book are named below their photos. Other images are stock photos from various photo libraries.

James Carlton Fussell

Preface

I wrote this book. Some of it's true. Some of it's not. We lived as poor people but most of the people that live in Okahumpka was as poor as we was. We all worked so we could eat. We lived hand to mouth. Even though we was poor people, we was happy.

A lot of the stories in the book really did happen. But it's a good thang my mama didn't know all we done. All the people in this book are my friends from way back and some are friends today. Even though we was poor and had very little, I wouldn't trade my life for one with a lot of money. I'm a better person and find my happiness in the friends I have around me.

Red Fussell

James Carlton Fussell

Skeeters and Hogs and Mules, Oh My!

Leesburg High School

Chapter 1

I were jist settin' on the porch lookin' at the chickens in the yard. They shore did look like they's havin' fun. They's scratchin' everythin' that the cats digged up. I'm tryin' to not thank 'bout school, cause we's gonna have to go to the big school in Leesburg. I shore don't wanna go there. Them big boys told us they have an 'lectric paddle. They make y'all bend over and then they turn on the switch. I don't want no part of that.

I told my mama I don't wanna go there. She jist looked at me. I knowed right then I gotta go, but that don't make me wanna go.

My mama works in the packin' house so she bought me 2 shirts, 2 pairs of pants and a new pair of shoes. I wear them Red Rider shoes most of the time. They's my favorite.

And she told me I gotta carry my lunch, 'cause it costs too much to eat in the lunch room. I don't care, but I shore don't wanna carry no s'rup bucket with my lunch in it. Them Leesburg kids make fun of us the way we look and talk as it is. I can jist hear 'em if'n we carry a s'rup bucket.

My mama made me take a bath on Sunday, so I'd be clean to go to school the next day. We caught the bus at Mr. Hall's store. They was a big boy in the seventh grade. He were 16 years old. When we got off the bus he sed, "Here come that white trash from Okahumpka." He were 'bout half right, but I didn't like it nohow. I told my friend Byron, "We should let 'im know 'bout white trash."

But Byron sed, "He's big and he'll beat y'all's eyes shut."

When the bus got to school, they told us what class to go to. They was 'bout 30 kids in the class. I knowed I warn't gonna like this at all.

I et my lunch out back at noon. I warn't the only one that brought lunch. Some had a lunch box, but most jist had a paper bag. Nobody brought a s'rup bucket. I shore was glad I didn't bring one.

When school were out, we caught the bus to go back home. They parked the bus in our yard, so now I can jist catch the bus at home. That were nice if'n it were a rainy day.

Ever' time that seventh grader that called us white trash seen us, he had some smart somethin' to say. I finally told Byron, "I've had 'bout all I'm gonna take from 'im." So when we got home on Friday, Byron and I went to Bugg Spring and cut us a green bamboo pole. Then we went to my dad's blacksmith shop, fired up the forge, and got some lead he made fishin' weights with. We melted the lead and got it ready to pour in the bamboo. I already knowed lead and water don't mix. When we poured the lead in, it come back out. We shouldn't a put it in green bamboo. It had a lot of water in it. We both looked like we'd been shot with a shot gun. We had burnt spots all over our faces. It wouldn't wash off, neither.

We went back to Bugg Spring and got us a dry bamboo stick. We heated the lead back up and poured the lead in this dry piece. It jist smoked. So I poured water on the bamboo to cool it off. Then I split the bamboo and taked the lead out and sawed off what I thought I needed afore I put out the fire in the forge. My dad kilt deer and tanned the hide, so I got me a piece of that leather from the deer and sewed the leather up with the lead in it. And I made a strap, so that seventh grader couldn't take it away from me. I double-stitched it jist like I seen my dad do.

I taked my new weapon outside 'cause I thought I needed to try it out. I thought 'bout hittin' the hog up the side of the head to see if'n it worked, then thought better of that idea. If'n my dad seen me do that, he'd use it on me.

Skeeters and Hogs and Mules, Oh My!

I taked my weapon to school the next day but that seventh grader didn't show up. I were really glad in a way, but if'n he calls us white trash 'gain, I'll show 'im what white trash is. I keeped that piece in my pocket all day and didn't show it to nobody.

The next day when we got to school, there he were. Byron looked at me and sed, "He's gonna beat y'all up so bad y'all's mama won't even know who y'all is."

When we stepped off the bus that seventh grader sed, "Here come the white..." He never got the word "trash" out 'cause I hit 'im right 'tween the eyes and a goose egg popped up. He went right to 'is knees.

I started to hit 'im again but Byron sed, "Don't kill 'im; he don't wanna fight."

I went on to class, but then seen Mr. Hayes tell the teacher somethin' and pointed right at me. I thought, *I shore hope I don't go to jail*. Mr. Hayes taked me to the office and wanted to see the blackjack. I showed it to 'im. He wanted to know who made it. I telled 'im I done it.

He first talked to the seventh grader and the seventh grader sed he were jist playin' 'round. That goose egg were still there. Mr. Hayes then telled the seventh grader he could go on to class. I jist knowed Mr. Hayes were gonna use that 'lectric paddle on me next, and thought I probably wouldn't have any behind left on me when he got done. But he asked me what happened. I telled 'im, "He kept callin' us white trash every day and I'd jist had 'nuff of it."

Mr. Hayes sed that seventh grader weren't all there and to stay away from 'im, and he sed, "Don't bring that thang back to school."

When I got back to class, everyone looked at me, but nobody sed nothin'. When we got on the bus, Byron asked me what happened. I telled 'im that Mr. Hayes put that 'lectric paddle on me and I didn't want no more of it.

I jist knowed someday that seventh grader would catch me off somewhere and beat the stuffin' out of me. So I taked 3 dollars out of the money I had and went to B.O. Harris Hardware store. I bought me a "Saturday night special" and a box of .22 shorts. It were a small gun I could put in my pocket. I shore hope I never need to use it.

'Bout 6 months later at the pool room, that boy walked up to me and sed, "I think' I'll whip y'all's butt."

I telled 'im, "I don't think so." And I pulled out the pistol.

He sed, "That's jist a toy."

I fired a round behind 'is feet in the pool room. They put me out of the pool room and told me not to come back. The seventh grader telled ever'body that I carried a piece and that I shot 'is foot. Well, 'if'n I'd shot 'is foot, I woulda hit it.

'Bout a week later I went back to the pool room and Frank let me in, but sed, "No guns."

I telled 'im, "Okay." But I carried that pistol till the day I went in the Army.

Teen-age Red   *Red Fussel*

A Trip to the Swamp

Chapter 2

The week were short at the big school. Warn't as bad as I thought it'd be. Friday I had got all my work done, and asked Byron if'n he'd wanted to go to the swamp on Saturday.

He sed, "Shore."

We hadn't been back to the swamp at all durin' the summer after Uncle Will died. We loved that ole black man, and when he died it 'bout broke my heart. And after he died, and we done kilt that big ole snake, the swamp jist warn't fun. There warn't nothin' excitin' goin' on. So it were time we went back.

I left the house 'bout 8 in the mornin'. He were ready to go. We walked down Stage Coach Road and walked by Uncle Will's ole house. We stopped. I felt like I jist wanted to cry.

Then Byron sed, "Wanta burn 'is house down?"

I hadda thank for a few minutes. Then I sed, "No. Maybe some-body'll move in it. But I'm shore he won't be like Uncle Will."

Then Byron sed, "Let's go to Lake Dunham Swamp."

I sed, "That's okay with me."

We waded in on the log we knowed 'bout. When we got to the platform, it looked jist like we left it when we caught that big ole snake.

Some of the junk we used was still there. We climbed up the ladder, laid on them hard boards and looked 'cross the sawgrass. Then I asked Byron, "I wonder...could they be 2 snakes?"

He sed, "I shore hope so."

We looked at the ole pine tree that died when lightnin' struck it.

We still had ole Joe's hide. We should try'n sell it.

We'd been there for 'bout 2 hours when out come a gator. I telled Byron to look over 'is right eye. Sed, "See, that's where I shot 'im one night when we was gator huntin'."

Gator   *Peg Urban*

Byron sed, "If'n it is, then we didn't kill ole Joe."

Sed, "Well, I never looked to see if'n Joe had been shot. So it could be ole Joe. He's a big gator. I guess Bill are still in jail. I kinda wish he were out to give us somethin' to worry 'bout."

We didn't even see that big ole hog. The swamp were quiet.

We left Dunham Swamp, stopped and pulled us some rabbit tobacco to smoke. We went to Cason Hammock, climbed up to our other tree house. It just didn't feel the same. We lit up our pipes. I looked up and there were Uncle Will's pipe nailed to the tree. I shore miss 'im, but we'd jist have to git used to it.

We climbed down and started home but stopped short. They were somethin' in the woods, but we didn't know what it were. It moved to the right of us, but we couldn't see it. It were comin' our way. We got ready to shoot if'n we had to. But out stepped the snake man. He were snake huntin'.

He sed, "Boys, it's me."

He were jist like us. He didn't have no shoes on.

He sed, "It shore is quiet after y'all kilt that big ole snake."

I told 'im that sometimes I wish we hadn't a kilt 'im, cause then we'd have somethin' to do now. But the snake man told us that snake probably woulda kilt somebody if'n he'd stayed alive. He were glad that snake were dead.

He sed, "The swamp shore are quiet. I never seen it this quiet."

I sed, "Maybe we have a bad storm comin'. Ever'thang beds up when a bad storm's a comin'. "

We walked to Stage Coach Road, waded 'cross the pond. The snake man went home. We decided to stop at the swing to swing some. Byron's little brother were there. He still had some green on 'is arms where we tested the dye afore dying the neighbor's mule on Halloween. Byron's oldest sister told us that when she hung 'round us, her mama whipped 'er behind. We jist laffed, but it were true.

I told Byron, "I'm gonna go home."

I left and started across the clay road. Well, guess who were there—the game warden. He wanted to know what we was shootin'.

I told 'im, "Nothin."

Then he told me, "Someday I'm gonna catch y'all boys and put y'all in jail."

I jist looked at 'im and walked off.

When I got home, I 'membered it were Saturday. And, yes, I hadda take a bath!

They didn't think much of us at the high school, but they didn't say a thang to me. They knowed I carried a gun. I never pulled it on no one, but they knowed I had it.

The rich kids looked down on the poor ones, or at least that's what we thought. As I look back, I were wrong.

The Night in the Swamp

Chapter 3

I got up Sunday mornin' and went to church. The preacher preached a long sermon. I thank he thought Byron and me needed it. Maybe we did.

We went to school all week but not much happened. It shore warn't like the little Okahumpka school where they was always somethin' happenin'. When Friday come 'round we sed we would spend the night in the tree house.

I left Friday afternoon. My mama gived me some flour and she had cooked some sweet taters. She put some in a paper sack for us. And she gived me some coffee. We could get the water out of the run. The water were clean, but we would boil it to make shore. Afore I left, she telled me to be careful.

We walked by Uncle Will's ole house. I asked Byron, "Do y'all thank they's boogers in there?"

He sed, "If'n they is, they'd be good boogers."

We both laffed. They ain't no boogers, I hope.

Afore dark we builded a fire and set there 'til the skeeters started eatin' us. We already set up camp in our tree house. So we climbed up and et the sweet taters after makin' shore we had our screens closed. They was a few skeeters inside, but we kilt 'em. As the dark closed in, the noise started. If'n y'all never spent a night in the swamp, it shore sounds bad. We had our guns so we could take care of anythang that come 'round. Them frogs was loud. They was all kinds of noise.

We left the fire goin' so we could see what were goin' on. We seen somethang in the shadows of the fire, so Byron got 'is .45-70 ready. It were jist an ole dog. I don't know what he were lookin' for, somethang to eat, probably.

We filled our pipes with rabbit tobacco and lit them up. Whew! Doggie! This was the life. We had it all. I bet them Yankees would give anythang to have what we got.

Rabbit Tobacco

We smoked our pipes 'til they went out. Our bed sack shore felt good. The next thang we knowed, it were daylight. But we waited 'til the sun come up 'cause them skeeters won't be as bad then.

We was jist layin' up there when Byron gave me the quiet sign. He raised the screen and shot. I asked 'im what he shot. It were a small pig, all alone. The pig were 'bout 40 pounds. So we hanged 'im up and skinned 'is hide off. We taked the guts out, built a big fire and got ready to put 'im on the grill.

I asked Byron, "Do y'all thank Uncle Will still has any of that sauce he used to use?"

He sed, "I don't know."

Sed, "I'm gonna go look."

I left for Uncle Will's house and there it were right on the shelf where he kept it. And while I were there I picked up the cookin' rack we used to use. It looked dirty, but the fire would clean it. While I were gone, Byron cut the hams off. The fire were ready and we put 4 rocks on it and then laid the rack on the rocks. Then we put the meat on the grill and cut a stick that would work to turn it over.

We was cookin' along and looked up. Here come Byron's oldest sister, Betty Jean, with his little brother, Larry. We had a fry pan and mixed some lard in the flour. My mama gived me 2 eggs and we put 'em in the flour too. We had one sweet tater and put that in and mixed it all together. We put a little lard in that cast iron fry pan and poured the mixture in the melted lard. It filled the pan. We put it over the fire with a piece of tin on top of the fry pan. Then we put hot ashes on top of the tin. That way our bread would brown on the top and the bottom. We cut a palmetto fan to put the sauce on. In 'bout 15 minutes, the tin were risin' up. I guess I put too much in the pan. Byron tasted a piece of meat. MMM! It were good. We looked at the bread and it looked real good too. We cut some palmetto fans to use as our plates. We wouldn't even have to wash 'em.

I shore wished Uncle Will were with us to help eat it.

Byron sed, "I bet he's lookin' down from Heaven at us."

We taked the bread off the fire. It shore looked good. The wood fire smelled good. Betty Jean cut the bread. It were done and brown on the top and brown on the bottom. I et a piece. MMM! It were real good.

We set there and had a good meal. Then the snake man come by. We tried to git 'im to eat. He had a piece of meat and then he left. We had enough left over to eat for all day. We throwed the pig guts in the bushes. Some varmint would eat 'em. We was like a big ole fat hog when they et. Then they sleep. We all climbed in the tree house and taked a nap, jist like the fat hogs done.

A Bad Trip to Leesburg

Chapter 4

It were jist a lazy Saturday. Not much to do. We decided to go to Leesburg and walk 'round. It were 'bout 9 o'clock in the mornin'. We stuck out our thumbs. A man from Center Hill picked us up. He were goin' to Lady Lake. So he dropped us off at Dixie Avenue in Leesburg and we walked up Dixie. We stopped at Smith Grocery Store.

Byron sed, "Let's git us a pint of wine and not pay for it." He hid it in 'is shirt. When we started out, Mr. Smith stopped us at the door and asked for the pint of wine. I shore were hopin' he wouldn't put us in jail.

But he took us to the back of the store and gived us a pan with soapy water. He told us to clean all the shelves and clean all the canned goods. We worked all that mornin' cleanin' shelves and all the canned goods. Then he told me to clean the bathroom. At noon he gived Byron and me a ham sandwich and a drink. We set in the back of the store to eat.

Mr. Smith then gived Byron a rake and he raked the back yard while I washed the front windows. After I finished with the windows, I helped Byron put all the leaves in garbage cans. Then we had to pick up all the trash around the store. Mrs. Smith gived us a cold drink and we 'membered to thank 'er for it. We then swept out the store room in the back.

By then it were 3 o'clock. Mr. Smith telled us to come to 'is office. He telled us we done a good job, and that he didn't want us to steal no more. If we wanted somethang we was to ask for it, but it were better to work for what we wanted. He telled us he were gonna pay us for the work we done. He even gived Byron a pint of wine and he gived me one too. I looked at it and thought, *I don't want it.*

Mr. Smith telled us, "Once a month I'd like y'all to work and clean the store."

When we went to leave I set my pint of wine by the door. I don't know what Byron done with 'is. We worked for Mr. Smith off and on for 'bout a year.

Even today, when I look at wine, I don't want none. I thank Mr. Smith done the right thang. If'n Uncle Will were still alive, he woulda been mad at us. He telled us he never stole nothin' and I'm shore he didn't.

The Pool Room

Chapter 5

We helped a man in 'is yard on Friday after school and he gived us six quarters. It warn't dark yet, so we went to the pool room to shoot a few games. The next thang we knowed, it were 'bout dark.

We left the pool room and I knowed I should already be home. We thought we'd walk the railroad tracks to git home. I knowed my mama warn't home yet. She were workin' in the packin' house. I'd still be home afore she got off work.

We started down the track on South Street. As we walked, it got darker and darker. We was goin' through the swamp close to Sawgrass Curve. Byron gived me the quiet signal and we stopped. Y'all could hear somebody comin' the other way. So we hid off to the side and squatted down.

Jist as he passed us, Byron jumped up and sed, "Shoot 'im!" Y'all could hear 'im runnin' down the railroad track. I thought it were funny 'til someone sed, "Who y'all gonna shoot?"

Then we run down the railroad track. I telled Byron, "That's the last time I'm walkin' the track at night!"

We stopped runnin' just a little ways down the track and had to stop to catch our breath. We could still hear 'im comin' down the track. We didn't know who it were, but we thought it would be best to let 'im go on by. They were jist enough light to see who he were when he went by us.

As he went by we knowed who he were. It were Ralph! He had a frog gig and he were frog huntin'. I guess 'is light had done gone out and he were tryin' to catch up with us to scare us.

We had 'im now. So we let 'im git a good ways down the track. Then we got a rock off the railroad bed and started beating on the track. He warn't comin' our way. I don't thank he knowed where we was at.

We was havin' fun. Then thangs got worse. We seen the train light. Now, the only way out was to git in the ditch with the snakes. I telled Byron, "How do we git in such messes?"

We got in the ditch. I'd rather be snake bit than have a train run over me where all I'd leave would be a mess!

The freight train went by. We quickly climbed out of the ditch. I telled Byron, "My mama is gonna kill me for messin' up my clothes."

We walked out on Hwy 27 and walked on to Okahumpka. When I got home I washed my pants to git the mud out, and tried to clean my shoes and socks. I hanged my clothes and shoes on the clothes line to dry.

When my mama seen them she washed 'em again. I telled 'er I got mud on them. She telled me the next time to change afore I git in the mud.

I thought, *She already knowed I'd been into somethin'.*

She worked hard so we could have some of the little thangs of life.
Red Fussell

Rain

Chapter 6

They were a dark cloud formin' from the south. My dad told me to tie the boat to the tree; he didn't want it to blow away or float away. I made the chickens go in the chicken house; some dumb chicks will stand in the rain and drown. Them hogs like the rain.

My mama had a rain barrel to catch water to wash 'er hair. So we poured out the water and cleaned the barrel. Then we put it back so it'd catch the rain water.

Dad cut some wood for the wood stove, then some for the fireplace. He nailed some tin over 2 windows on the south side and turned the rockin' chairs so they wouldn't get blowed away. Then the rain come!

I told my dad, "I'm goin' to the barn."

But he told me, "No. This-here's gonna be a bad storm."

The thunder and lightnin' come in bunches. The old house leaked, so they put pots and pans to catch the water. My mama started cookin' some greens and some corn bread. She told me, "If'n it's a bad storm, it could last for days."

The wind blowed. I never seen it rain so hard. The dog got under the house; the cat moved inside. My brother didn't go nowhere. They moved ever'thang from under the big oak in the yard and we all went to bed. I went to sleep so don't know what it done. When I waked up it were still rainin' and the rain barrel were full of water. The wind were blowin' the trees all around. My dad fed the chickens and fed the hogs. He gived some bones to the dog and my mama gived the cat some corn bread.

Mama made some biskets and we had some cane s'rup. She fried eggs and fixed a pot of grits. I could eat this ever' day.

The wind blowed till 'bout 3. Then it stopped. My dad told Lewis Jr. to git the rod and reels. Sed, "The fish should be in the ditches of clear lake water."

We rided down to the ditches. He were right. We caught a bunch of fish.

Then he told us. "Let's git back home."

The rain had come back with a lot of rain and it rained all day long. We cleaned the fish on the porch. My mama fried 'em up. MMM. They shore was good. Mama had put the fish grease on the grits.

It were 'bout dark and we all went to bed. When I waked the next day it were still rainin'. The yard had water standin' all over it. I asked my mama where my dad had gone and she told me he'd gone to feed the mules on Merritt Road. I shore hoped he'd made it okay.

'Bout an hour later he come back. He were wet and sed that water were over the road on Highway 27.

It rained all day. Ever'thang were wet! We set 'round the stove in the kitchen to stay warm and et some cold biskets with some guava jelly. My! They was good along with some cold fish.

It rained 2 more days and ever'where y'all looked they were water. My dad told us to watch out for snakes.

Then Dad wanted the chicken house cleaned out. The chickens would git sick if'n it warn't cleaned out. He went to go check on the hogs and feed 'em. As soon as it cleared up he got back to plowin' to git rid of the grass.

Byron come over and sed, "They's no need to go to the swamp. Ever'thang's under water." But we walked down Highway 27. The road were under water, but we still walked right down the road. It were 'bout knee deep.

The next day Byron come over with Betty Jean, Melba and Larry.

Skeeters and Hogs and Mules, Oh My!

We stopped by Catfish's house and he come along. We was gonna wade down Highway 27. We was wadin' when Byron dropped to 'is knees. He sed, "Look, they's a hole here!" We all laffed.

Then a car come by and the woman sed, "Is there a hole there?"

We pitched it up and sed, "They shore is!"

Then Catfish sed, "They's 'nother hole jist down the road."

He told 'em, "For 25 cents we'll lead y'all through."

She sed, "We don't wanna run in no hole in the road." So she gived 'im the money.

Catfish told Larry to git in the hole over farther and to drop to 'is knees like he were in a hole. The lady drove 'round 'im!

That shore were fun! We left and went to the store and got us 3 of them Black Cow candy bars.

We was chewin' on them when guess who were on the road! The highway policeman were there and seen us. He told us to come over to 'im. The woman done called 'is office and reported that they was bad holes in the road. We jist looked at 'im.

He asked Byron where them holes was. Byron sed, "There ain't no hole in the road."

The policeman sed, "Y'all boys have been at it again!"

Then Catfish sed, "Here's a hole." He were on 'is knees.

Byron and me run across the field by a big ole house. We knowed we warn't gonna git caught but, we had-a stay out of 'is way, 'cause he'd be lookin' for us. I shore hoped he didn't know our names.

Catfish got away from 'im, but I don't know how.

We stayed away from the store for a while, and the main road, too. My dad asked me what I'd been doin'.

Sed, "Nothin'. Jist been wadin' on the highway." I knew he knowed what we'd done, but I acted like I didn't know what he were talkin' 'bout.

The Gofer Hole

Chapter 7

It were jist one of 'em lazy days when they's not much to do. I asked Byron if'n he wanted to go to the creek up by the bridge. He did. So we started down the railroad track, then headed toward Sawgrass Lake. It were a good walk, but we had plenty of time. We stopped and et some oranges. We seen a big rat snake, but we left 'im alone cause rat snakes keep the rattlesnakes away. Jist a little way down the dirt road, I seen a big rattlesnake. We guessed he were 'bout 5 or 6 feet long. He didn't coil up; he run down the gopher hole, so we caved it in.

Then we went to the snake man's house and told 'im they were a big snake in that hole. So he got 'is sack and 'is shovel. He were gonna dig 'im out. We'd never seen 'im do that. We got on the back of 'is Model A Goat. He had a sack to put the snake in and a stick to catch that big ole snake. We showed 'im where to go.

When we got to that hole, we set on the back of that Goat to be out of 'is way. I warn't gonna dig no rattlesnake nest. I didn't know how many was in there or how big they was. But we knowed that one we seen were big. That gopher hole made a turn on the bottom. The dirt were soft so it warn't hard to dig, and soon snake man digged down to where the turn were. He hadn't found even one snake yet but we knowed it were there. Then all of a sudden the snake man jumped out of that hole and grabbed that-there stick he catches snakes with, and he backed off. He told us they was 2 snakes in the hole, and one of them snakes were mad. We could hear 'im rattle. They called it singin' and he were doin' a real good job of it.

He tied a string on a stick and made a loop. Then he walked back up to the hole and reached in, put the loop over the snake's head and pulled up. He had the snake! The snake man told us to brang 'im the bag to put the snake in. I told Byron, "I ain't a gonna mess with no rattlesnake!"

Byron got the bag and the snake man told Byron to hold the bag. It were a big snake! He put the tail in first and then the head. Then he grabbed the top and tied a string 'round the top. He told us they were 'nother snake in the hole, but he'd take this one home first and would be right back. Afore he left, he sed, "Don't let that other snake run away!"

Rattlesnake

Now, how was we gonna keep that snake from runnin' away? Well, the snake man warn't gone long. He had a different stick this time. He told us, "This-here's a big snake in that hole."

He tapped the snake on the head, and that made 'im coil up. I guess if'n y'all tapped me on the top of my head, I'd coil up too. He had a hard time gittin' the loop over the snake's head. But he finally got it. I

19

asked Byron if'n he were gonna hold the sack again.

He sed he would, but not me! He held the sack so the snake man could put the snake in it. Then the snake man told us they was some-thin' else in the hole. We was lookin' in the hole when out flew an owl! He warn't very big, but I fell on the ground. I thought shore it were 'nother snake. I didn't know that owls would stay with rattlesnakes in the same hole. Then the snake man told us, "Y'all can find all kinds of thangs in the gofer holes." He sed that sometime they'll be 2 or 3 rattle-snakes in one hole. I asked 'im, "Have y'all ever been bit by a snake?"

He sed, "No."

That's all the snake man done for a livin'. When he snake-hunted, he didn't even wear no shoes. He sed they hurt 'is feet. I guess he's right, cause we didn't have no shoes on our feet neither.

We walked on down to the creek and put our feet in the water. It were cool. The day'd been fun, but I ain't gonna catch no snake like that. I asked Byron, "Was y'all scared?"

He sed, "Yes."

We walked back home. It were supper time. Them oranges had gived out a long time ago and my stomach were a-growlin'.

My mama asked me what me what I done today. I telled 'er, "Jist played 'round."

I washed my face and washed my feet and washed my hands. We et supper and I went to bed.

Fishin' Trip to Homosassa

Chapter 8

I were settin' on the porch watchin' 'em toads and frogs catch bugs. The man from Leesburg drived up and wanted to know if'n we wanted to go fishin' like we done afore. I telled 'im, "Yes! But I have to ask Byron."

I seen Byron Saturday and asked 'im if'n he wanted to go fishin' in the Gulf like we done one other time. He sed, "Shore would."

The next Saturday we was ready at 5 in the mornin'. I had my hat, my shoes, a long sleeved shirt, a bandana to cover my face and a pair of gloves. He always had all the drink we could hold, and lunch. We got in Homosassa jist at day break. It shore looked good. The man at the dock telled us it might be rough and to jist watch the wind.

When we left marker 2 there warn't no wind. And it were hot! The man put us out on a rock bed. The fish was bitin' real good. They was some big fish and plenty of 'em. It were fun! We fished the rock bed for 'bout an hour. Then he moved to 'nother rock bed. The fish was a nice size there too.

It were 'bout 12 so we et lunch. He had a good lunch. Then we rested some afore goin' back to fishin'. It were fun, but he kept lookin' at a black cloud in the southwest. The water got a little rough, so he telled us to roll up the poles 'cause we needed to git back. We started back to marker 2. It were rough and the boat were bouncin'. I felt funny and put my head over the side of the boat. Then I chummed the fish with what I ate. I let it all go. I looked over at Byron and he were chummin' the other side.

Wind had got high and rain were pourin' down the pump. The pump were pumpin' the water out the boat. We went past marker 2 and was goin' down the river. Then lightnin' struck a tree on the right side of the boat. I thought I felt it, but I warn't shore. When we arrived at the fish camp, ever'thang were wet. We put the fish in 'is box and cleaned the boat. I didn't feel bad once I stepped on the dock. I got me a drink and then I felt better.

We put the fish in 'is car and walked in the fish house. The man in the fish house told us that 2 men had been struck by lightnin' and was kilt. They was bringin' 'em to the dock. I didn't care to see that. When they brought 'em in, they was wrapped, so we didn't see. I guess that coulda been us.

We left the dock to go home. He stopped at a hamburger place to git us a hamburger, some French Fries and a drink. They shore was good. We had a bunch of fish that we done caught. When we got back in Okahumpka he gave us a big fish each. And he asked if'n we wanted to go again. We told 'im, "Shore! But we hope it don't storm!"

Skeeters and Hogs and Mules,
Oh My!

The Otter Trap

Chapter 9

I stopped by Byron's to ask if'n he could go over to Lake Dunham Swamp, but he couldn't go. So I had my .22 and a box of shells and eased 'round the orange grove by myself. I seen somethang move, but warn't shore what I seen. I checked the tracks and still didn't know what it were.

So I eased down next to the swamp and seen it were an otter, and it were big!! I raised to shoot it, but it were real fast. I looked 'round and they were a slide where he went in the small pond.

I went back to Byron's to tell 'im what I seen, and told 'im I'd need a trap to catch it. So we made our plan to go then to Leesburg on Saturday to git a trap.

We hopped the 11 o'clock train in Okahumpka, hopped off in Leesburg, and walked down to B.O. Harris Hardware Store. He had 'bout ever'thang in 'is store. We walked inside and B.O sed, "Well, boys, what do y'all need?"

I telled 'im, "I need a trap to catch an otter."

He telled me it would cost one dollar and fifty cent, and he then showed me how to set the trap. He telled me I'd need a chain.

I sed, "What do I need a chain for?"

He told me I had to nail the chain to a tree. I needed to have a tree cut off so I could put a window weight on the stump and wire it to the chain. When the otter runs with the trap it'll drown 'im. He even sed the otter would bite 'is foot off if'n he warn't dead, to git rid of the trap, and they can even turn in they's skin. B.O. sed, "I thank the best thang to do is to leave that-there otter alone!"

Well, I handed 'im the money and he taked it. Then B.O. sed, "Don't tell y'all's dad y'all bought that-there trap here."

I asked 'im for a sack to put it in. The sack he gived me looked like a feed sack.

We left the hardware store and walked down Dixie Ave. When we got to 27, we stuck out our thumbs to catch a ride back to Okahumpka. We catched one real quick.

Another thang B.O. telled us when he sold us the trap were that when we skin the otter, he has a stink sack under 'is front legs. Well, we done been sprayed once by a polecat. We knowed all 'bout smell, and we didn't need no more of that.

I telled Byron Sunday after church that we needed to set that trap for the otter. He asked me what we was gonna do with 'im. I telled 'im, "The man that buys gators buys otters, too. I don't know how much, but I thank it's a bunch."

We went to church. After church I et a quick lunch, grabbed the sack with the trap, a hammer, and a window chain with some wire. And I had my prunin' saw. We both done changed our clothes and taked off our shoes. We knowed we'd git wet and muddy. We walked by Uncle Will's old house. Somebody were livin' in there. He were an old grouch so we didn't stop. We didn't like 'im much.

We was walkin' through the grove and Byron sed, "They's the big snake track!" It were a snake track 'bout one inch wide. We both laffed.

We went down to where the slide were and we sawed the tree top off 'bout 6 inches out of the water, jist like B.O. sed to do. Then we set the trap.

I telled Byron, "He slides down 'is slide."

We put the window weight on it. I taked the chain and nailed it to a big tree. We hid the chain in the water and put a stick so he'd go straight in the trap. We was gonna be trappers. We done kilt that big snake, and now was gonna catch otters and make a bunch of money.

Skeeters and Hogs and Mules, Oh My!

Monday when we got out of school, we taked off to the swamp. The trap were sprung, but no otter. We reset the trap and moved our stick in it so he'd have to go in the trap.

My brother had bought a single barrel shotgun, a 20 gauge. I shore did like it. So the next day I slipped it out along with 5 shells, and stopped by Byron's. I sed, "Let's go see what's in the trap."

We walked by Uncle Will's ole house. The grouchy man told us, "Git off my property and don't y'all come back!"

I sed, "What we need to do one night is to string 'is house with a rosen ball." We laffed.

Otter Eating Fish   *Peg Urban*

We walked down Stage Coach Road and down through the orange groves. Then we walked to where the trap were set. It were gone! The window weight were gone! I put a shell in the shot gun and taked off my clothes so I wouldn't get wet. I pulled on the chain and up he come. That otter were showin' 'is teeth. I grabbed 'hold that shot gun and poked the barrel in the mud. When I turned 'round he were comin' at me! I pulled the trigger and that gun kicked like a cracker mule that time we put that pine cone under the horse's tail!

I don't know what that otter done but when I threwed the gun down the barrel were split back 'bout 6 inches. My shoulder had done turned blue already. We seen the otter were tryin' to git air but the weight held 'im down in the water. We stayed there and watched 'im die.

Byron sed, "What's Lewis gonna say when he sees 'is gun?"

I sed, "I could give 'im the otter hide. He should be able to buy a new one with that."

We drug the outter out, hit 'im in the head with a stick to make shore he were dead. Then we skinned 'im out and sold the skin for 15 dollars, so we bought Lewis a new gun. We even had 6 dollars left over.

I asked Byron, "Should we buy more traps with what we got left?"

When I told my dad what we'd done he jist laffed. Then he wanted to know how my arm were. It were blue and still hurt.

One Saturday night I stayed at Byron's house. We went to the grouchy man's house where Uncle Will used to live and we stringed 'is house. We pulled the string as tight as we could and Byron taked the rosen ball. When he pulled the ball on the string it even scared me and I knowed what it were.

Then we left the string lay there and we waited till we thought he were asleep. We done it again. When the light went on in the house, we went back to Byron's house and went to bed.

The next day one of the women from the Quarters was chantin' and beatin' the ole house with a white cloth.

Byron and me sed we'd have to do that again some time.

The Snake Man

Chapter 10

The weeks passed fast. School done started. I asked Byron if'n he'd like to go talk to the snake man, Mr. George, to see if'n he'd seen that big ole hog.

He said, "Shore."

So we walked down the clay road to Mr. George's house. It were jist a place, a cracker house, jist a place to git in out of the rain. But it had a fire place to stay warm. Jist 'bout all 'em ole houses had fire places. And jist 'bout ever'body could cut wood.

He were settin' on the porch and waved at ever' body that went by. We walked up and he told us to come on in. So we set on the porch with 'im. We asked 'im if'n he'd seen that big ole hog.

He sed he shore had. He were over by the island lookin' for snakes when he looked up and there were that hog. Sed, "I climbed a plum tree when that hog run at me. Then the hog walked 'round and 'round the tree. I thought he never would leave! Then all at once he runned off, and I heerd somethang I ain't never heerd afore, but I knowed I had to git out of the swamp! When I walked down Stage Coach Road it felt like somebody were follerin' me. I never did see nothin' but I knowed it were there!"

We didn't say nothin'. He told us it'd be best to stay out of that swamp. Sed, "No tellin' what kind of booger's in there!"

Byron and I jist looked at each other. We thought it may be that-there cat. It were big and smart. I were more skeered of that cat than I were the snake. We seen 'im once when we was after the snake.

We thought maybe we should tell Mr. Richer, the game warden, 'bout the cat. Then we sed, "No, we may have to kill 'im; and we shore don't wanna go to jail for killin' 'im."

I don't know how fast that cat can run, but I knowed we can't out-run or out-climb 'im. We was told one time that it could slip up on us and we'd never know it.

We left Mr. George's house and went back to Byron's house. I telled Byron that we shore don't wanna go to the swamp without our guns! That night I dreamed how we was gonna catch that-there cat. My brother shaked me and wanted to know what were wrong.

I telled 'im, "Nothin'". But he knowed better.

A Skeered Trip to the Swamp

Chapter 11

Byron and me talked it over and decided that next Saturday we'd go to the swamp. I asked my brother if'n I could borrow 'is 20-gauge shotgun.

He sed, "Ok. But if'n you tear it up, you gotta buy me a new one."

The next week I went to B.O. Harris' store to git me a box of 20-gauge high brass double-out-buck shotgun shells. *That should stop that hog, I hope.* I asked Byron if'n he'd like to spend the night in Cason Hammock.

He asked me, "Thank we should?"

Then I told 'im we'd put up a piece of tin so nothin' could git to us in the tree house. I told my mama I were gonna to spend the night in the swamp, and she told me to be careful and to stay up in our tree house. She gave me some sweet taters she'd cooked and a bag of other stuff. We left Byron's house 'bout dark, jist in time to build a big fire when we got to the tree house.

It were a dark night, but the fire would give us some light. We fried them sweet taters like pancakes, real crisp, and poured some cane syrup on them. They shore was good. Uncle Will taught us that.

I know what he'd say if'n he were alive. He'd say, "Stay outta that swamp!" He mighta been right.

We set 'round the fire 'til daylight were 'bout gone. Then we climbed the ladder. We knowed better'n to leave our guns on the ground. The night were cool, so we wrapped up in an old blanket we had. We got it from Uncle Will's house when he died. It still smelt like 'im. The night were still, but in the swamp they was all kinds of noises. Some sound bad, too. We'd heerd 'em all afore, and we went to sleep.

Then Byron shaked me and I waked up. He sed, "Somethang's climbin' this-here tree!"

All I could thank of were that cat!!!

I turned the shot gun where I thought he would climb. We set there real quiet. When I seen 'is eyes I shot! The noise was real loud. Then ever'thang done got quiet. I telled Byron, "I blowed 'is head off! I seen 'is eyes. Then I shot!"

Well, I shot a hole in the screen too, so we stuffed part of the blanket in the hole.

Byron asked me, "Do you wanna climb down to see what it were?"

I sed, "No! It's dark."

We could hear a noise on the ground but couldn't see nothin'. We'd jist wait till day light.

Byron sed, "Let's go back to sleep."

I did go to sleep, and when we waked up the sun were shinin'. We loaded our guns and climbed down to see what we'd killed, but it were all gone. All that were left were blood. We looked for tracks, but didn't find no fresh tracks.

We looked ever'where, but no tracks. It'd be hard to find track if'n it were small. We didn't even know what it were, but we knowed it were dead now.

We flattened out 2 sweet taters, jist like Uncle Will showed us how. We fried bacon first so we could git the lard to fry them sweet patties. We fried 'em taters 'til they was crisp, then poured cane s'rup on them. MMMM! They was good!

Byron sed, "Let's go to the swamp."

So we packed up ever'thang and walked through the grove. We walked the log in and climbed up on our platform. We laid there for 'bout an hour. Then I seen Old Joe, the gator. I were shore that were 'im. He had a crease right where I shot 'im a long time ago.

He swimmed by, but I'm shore he looked right at us when he passed by. Maybe he thought we was somethin' to eat.

We'd been there quite a while when Byron touched me to be quiet. I looked over where he were pointin'; the bushes was shakin'. We got ready. If'n it were that big old hog, we'd shoot 'im. But out come a dog. Guess he were huntin' somethang to eat. Ever'thang's gotta eat. The dog didn't see us, but the bushes kept shakin'. We knowed it weren't no hog, but out stepped a man. He lived in Uncle Will's old house. We didn't say a word.

The dog waited in the swamp and the man follered 'im. We jist laid still. I bet he were lookin' for a hog. He didn't know 'bout the log. We laid there for a little longer and then that there dog bayed up. You could tell he had somethang. We didn't know what, but then we heerd the dog fightin'. He squealed and then it were quiet. But the man then screamed, "HELP!" Maybe the hog got 'im!

We hollered, "Where y'all at?"

He hollard, "Over here!"

We knowed where he were. We made shore our guns was loaded. I'd hate to fight a hog with no shells in the gun. When we got there he were up a tree holdin' on for dear life. Byron asked 'im what were wrong.

He sed, "That-there big old hog kilt my dog and put me up the tree."

Byron asked, "Where's y'all's gun?"

It were on the ground. We done that one time, but never again!

When he climbed down he were shakin'. That hog almost got 'im. If'n 'is dog hadn't a-run at 'im, he woulda got 'im.

I asked 'im, "What was y'all doin' in the swamp?"

He sed, "I were hog huntin', but I won't come back down here."

He were wet up to 'is shoulders. He sed, "They's too much mud and a bad hog!"

We hoped he wouldn't come back neither.

We walked out in the grove with 'im and walked down Stage Coach Road. He didn't even say, "Thank Y'all!" He jist walked into 'is house. Next time, we'll jist leave 'im up the tree!

We waded across the pond. The pond water kinda washed our feet.

I telled Byron, "I thank I'll go home. Maybe next Saturday we can do somethang."

When I got home my family were goin' to town. I didn't wanna go. I went out back and got one of them pigs. They's fun to play with. But that ole' sow gets mad if'n the little pigs squealed.

I taked my bath when ever'body were gone and then laid on the porch and taked a nap.I dreamed 'bout that big ole snake!

Jist One of Them Saturdays

Chapter 12

They warn't much goin' on at school and Saturday were a comin' up. Byron and me was tryin' to thank what we could do. We tried to find a job, but they were jist nothin' goin' on.

We didn't wanna go swing, so we walked down to the creek. Betty Jean come along, but the water were cold. We found a fish bed. It looked full of bluegills, so we went back to Okahumpka and got a fishin' pole and some hooks and line. Then we found a burned wasp nest. We opened the nest and got the larva out. It were good size, so we brought a piece of wire to string them blue gill fish on.

Byron gived Betty Jean the pole and put some bait on it. She dropped it in the hole and she got a fish real quick. It were a bass, but not big enough to keep. So he put bait on the hook again and she dropped it in and caught a nice blue gill. Byron and I didn't fish; we jist watched Betty Jean catch blue gills until we had a stringer full. So we got us a long stick and hung them fish on it and started to Byron's house.

A man stopped us on the way and wanted to know if'n we would sell 'em. We asked 'im how much he'd give us.

He sed, "One dollar."

We sed, "No." And we started to walk on.

So he sed, "Two dollars."

We sed, "No."

Then he sed, "Four dollars."

We telled 'im we'd take the 4 dollars, and we put the fish in the trunk of 'is car while he went to git the money outta 'is car. But he closed the door and drived off with our fish and our money! Now we was mad! Byron sed that guy hanged around the beer joint nearby and some day we'd catch 'im there.

About 2 weeks later we seen 'is car at the beer joint, so we was tryin' to thank what we should do. We thought 'bout lettin' the air out of 'is tires and maybe give 'im a tank of water. Then Byron sed we should take the hose and turn it on in the car. If'n he stayed in the beer joint, the car would fill up. So we done it, and then we left.

We didn't know how long he stayed in the beer joint but the water filled over the seats so we knowed he had a wet behind when he were goin' home. We shoulda filled 'is gas tank with water too.

We didn't see 'im for a long time, but the barman in the beer joint sed he were mad. Then we telled 'im what the man done to us. Barman sed he'd talk to 'im.

The next time we seen the man in the beer joint, he gave us our 4 dollars. We asked 'im what the barman sed to 'im, and he telled us the barman were gonna talk to the KKK.

The Maypop Vines

Chapter 13

When we got off the bus from school, a man come by our house. He wanted to know if'n Byron and me would like to pull Maypop vines. So I went over to Byron's house to see if'n he could go. The man told us he'd bring lunch. I shore were glad of that. It ain't hard work, but it's hot.

He picked us up at my house real early the next day and we went south of Groveland to a pasture. It were a big ranch. It were still pretty damp, so we waited 'til it were dried out a little. When the Maypop is ripe it looks dried up, but it tastes good. It jist has lots of seeds.

They take the vines and sell them. He had a side board on 'is trailer so we could put more vines on it. They was easy to pull. Some of them Maypops was green. I tried to eat 'em, but they warn't good. They shore was a lot of them there.

We pulled vines 'til lunch time. They was a bunch on that trailer, but they was still lots of vines in the fence row. We stopped for lunch. He bringed us six ham sandwiches and a big piece of cake. I don't know what kind, but it shore were good. And he had lots to drink. I et too much. We rested a bit and then went back to pullin' and loadin' the trailer.

Then I seen Byron run so I knowed somethin' were wrong. He run to where we was at and I asked 'im what were wrong. He had a spot on 'is arm where a yellow jacket stinged 'im. The man we was workin' for chewed a cigarette and put it on Byron's arm to stop the hurt. It worked. Byron telled 'im they was a big nest where he were standin'.

The man that owned the land drived up 'bout then. We telled 'im 'bout the yellow jacket nest. He telled us he'd be right back. He come back soon with 5 gallons of gas in two buckets. I'd seen my dad burn out a nest, but not with gas.

He throwed the gas on the nest and got the axe out from the back of 'is truck. He cut some splinters off the lighter stump. He had a big handful. I telled Byron, "I'm gonna back up. When he lights it, no tellin' where them flames'll go."

He lighted the splinters and threw them on the gas. It made a big noise. We had blue stuff all over us. I'm shore if any of them yellow jackets was still alive, they'd be mad!

The man that set them on fire were laffin'. He had dirt all over 'im. Then the man that we was workin' for telled us to go back to work.

We loaded the trailer and it were full. It were 'bout 5 o'clock, so the man sed it were time to quit. We got a drink and drinked all the way home. When we got home, the man telled us he would pay us when he sold the vines. I looked at Byron and he sed, "Ok."

It wouldn't be the first time we didn't get paid. The man left and we set on the porch. We was both lookin' at the ground. I telled Byron, "We'll never see 'im again."

Byron sed, "We shore won't work for 'im no more."

Byron left and walked home. I washed up and went to bed. My brother come in 'bout 12 o'clock. I were still awake thinkin' 'bout not gittin' paid.

The next day my brother wanted to know what were wrong. He sed I wiggled all night. I telled 'im we worked all day and he didn't pay us. Lewis jist sed, "Sometimes it happens."

When we went to school that Monday I were still mad, and so were Byron. When the bus stopped at the store after school, I got off with Byron. The man that we worked for were there. He sed, "Boys, come here."

We walked over there. I thought shore he were gonna tell us he couldn't pay us. I were mad at 'im. Byron and me could whip 'im. Then he sed, "Y'all boys work good. I sold them vines for 5 dollars and y'all can split it." That were good pay for a day with lunch.

Then he telled us, "If'n I find some more Maypop vines, I'll need help."

I shore were glad he paid us. I were savin' my money to git me one of them .20-gauge shotguns like my brother has.

Maypop vines   *Peg Urban*

Gulf Fritillarie butterflies use Maypop (aka Passion-vine) as their host plant to lay eggs on. The eggs hatch into orange, spiny caterpillars which feed on the leaves until they pupate (form a chrysalis). In about a week the transformed caterpillar emerges as a beautiful bright orange butterfly with shimmery silver patches on the underside of the wings. Several broods are hatched in the spring and summer, and the butterfliess reach peak populations from August through November in the South.

Peg Urban

The Raft

Chapter 14

We'd been down on the edge of the swamp but they warn't much goin' on even there. So we climbed up into our tree house. All we seen were one bird. We shore do miss that big ole snake. And we miss Uncle Will. We laff sometimes 'bout 'im gittin' drunk on that wine we made. And we stole 'is chicken and he cooked it for us.

Then Byron sed, "Let's build us a better raft."

So we climbed down and walked off down to Bugg Spring.

I told Byron, "I'm goin' home to git my prunin' saw." We had a roll of wire like they put on hay bales and I needed the saw to cut it.

When I got back to Bugg Spring, Byron warn't there. I walked to Byron's house and 'is mama told me he had to go help 'is dad move some logs, but should be back soon.

Well, it were gittin' late so I left and went home. I asked my dad to sharpen my saw. It didn't take long and it would cut real good now. He asked me what were I gonna do with it.

I told 'im, "Byron and me are gonna build a raft better'n we built afore."

He jist sed, "Watch y'all's weather for a good day to go sailin'."

The next day were Sunday. We jist got our stuff together when Byron's sister wanted to know what we was gonna do. We telled 'er we was goin' to Leesburg on the raft after we built it. Then Betty Jean wanted to go with us. Well, Byron didn't care as long as she helped us build it first.

When Saturday come 'round we was ready to cut 'bout 10 big bamboo stems. They was 'bout 30 feet long. And we done jist like Uncle Will telled us how to build it. We wired them next to each other and we turned the small ends over on the front of the float. Then we had the limb we cut off on top of the float and we cut small bamboo and put them on top of the float. We wired all this stuff real good. We even made a keel to guide it.

Then Sonny and 'is sister come up and they wanted to know what we was gonna do with the float. We telled 'em we was gonna float to Leesburg and push-pole it back.

Sonny sed, "I hope y'all make it."

Sonny's sister sed she wanted to go, but with all that weight we didn't thank it would hold 4 people. Sonny sed she must be crazy and sed, "That thang won't even float."

We was gittin' too many people involved in it. Then we installed two big bamboo on the top on each side. We got three push poles and we wired the rudder in place. We finally got it to work. What we was gonna do was two of us push and one steer. We pushed it into the spring. It floated real good, so we jumped on. Betty Jean had a time gittin' on, but with some pushin' and some pullin' we got 'er aboard.

We 'bout had to pole push and paddle 'til we got to Bugg Spring. It run good with the rudder. We taked it to where we keeped the boat. The bottom of Bugg Spring had deep mud and our poles sticked in the mud. It taked quite a bit of work to get the raft on the bank. I don't thank we woulda got it on the bank if'n Betty Jean hadn't abeen there. It shore looked good. The front were not as high as the first float. Maybe the wind wouldn't git us. The rudder were in good shape.

We made us a white flag so if'n we git blowed over we can call for help with the flag. Byron telled Betty Jean she hadda wear 'er bathin' suit 'cause when she gits wet, she looks like she has no clothes on. She sed she'd do that.

I taked the pole home with me and asked my dad what I could put on the pole so it wouldn't go in the mud. He told me to take it to the barn so he could look at it. He looked real good and then he picked up an old hinge. He taked 'is hammer, bent the hinge and bolted it to the bamboo. He told me that would work.

I went to Byron's house and told 'im my dad had bent 'im a hinge for 'is pole too. We drilled a hole and put it on. Then we cut 2 more poles to paddle. We was ready for Saturday. I were lookin' forward to it more and more.

When we got off the school bus, I telled Byron, "See y'all Saturday."

I were ready to go. I walked over to Byron's house Saturday mornin' but he had to help 'is dad. Now it would be next week afore we could go.

Betty Jean wanted to go to the swamp and work on the float. I needed to git my .22 first, jist in case a snake come out. When I got back to Byron's, Betty Jean were ready to go.

We taked the push poles to see how they work. When we got to the float it were in good shape. We retied some of them wires and tied wires where we didn't tie afore. When we finished there warn't nothin' else to do. So we walked by the tree house. Ever'thang looked good there. Then we walked down to Lake Dunham Swamp. We walked on the log that led to the spring and we went through the woods. The spring were flowin' real good.

I telled Betty Jean that there were someone at the spring. I could hear 'em talkin'. So we eased up close as we could without bein' seen. I seen a man and a woman that warn't 'is wife!

So I telled Betty Jean, "We best git outta here!"

Betty Jean sed, "I'm gonna holler at them!" And she done it!

I wanted to run, but I didn't. They run and jumped in they's car and taked off. She thought it were funny, but I didn't.

We walked back to Byron's house and he were home. He wanted to go to Bugg Spring Run where the raft were to see what we done. Betty Jean come along. It looked real good. Maybe next week we can make the trip.

I telled Byron, "I thank Ole Joe is still alive. I thank we should stay out of Lake Dunham. He's big and bad!"

Saturday come 'round fast. They wasn't many goin' on at school. Friday night I spent the night at Byron's house and we bought 6 cans of sardines so if'n we git hungry we'd have somethin' to eat on the trip.

Skeeters and Hogs and Mules, Oh My!

We got up early, et some eggs for breakfast that Betty Jean fixed for us. We got ready to leave. Betty Jean had her bathin' suit in a bag.

We waded 'cross the pond behind Byron's house and then down Stage Coach Road by Uncle Will's old house. We didn't see nobody. The man who lived there may have moved after all the noise we gived 'im. We walked by the tree house. I shore do like it. And we walked the cow trail to the float. We eased it in Bugg Spring Run. It shore looked good.

We put our poles on the float and our paddles. Them paddles was shorter than our poles. Then Betty Jean put on 'er bathin' suit and then 'er dress over it. We was ready to go. Betty Jean didn't wanna steer, so she used a push pole. The poles worked real good. I were steerin'. Some of the places had short curves so it were hard to git 'round. We seen a snake, but let it go by. Another time we woulda kilt it.

We warn't makin' real good time. We finally made it to Helena Run. It's wider. Maybe we could make better time. We was goin' a little faster. We got a little too close to the bank and stirred up a wasp nest when we went by. One stinged me.

Then Byron sed, "If'n I had some snuff I'd spit on it!" All we could do was laff 'bout it. We eased on down Helena Run and heerd a boat comin'. We got as close to the bank as we could. When the boat-man seen us, he slowed down and he jist laffed!!

He told 'is wife, "Look at 'em crazy kids."

Then he asked, "Where y'all goin'?

Betty Jean told 'im, "To Leesburg."

He sed, "Have fun."

I asked 'im if'n he had a cigarette and he sed he shore did.

So then I told 'im I got stinged and needed to put somethang on the sting. He gave me a little bottle and sed to put that stuff on it. I done it and the sting went away!

Then he gave us a candy bar. We thanked 'im and we was on our way again.

The bridge were a sight to see. We went under the new bridge.

Helena Run were a lot wider but the bottom had more mud. We was still gonna go to Leesburg. We could see the lake. The wind were not blowin' as hard as it were the last time we pushed in Lake Harris.

We stayed close to the edge. We'd found out how to push it real good. Some boats would go by and wave at us. That made us feel good. We was makin' good time now. We stopped on the edge of the lake to eat us a can of sardines. They shore was good. We washed our hands and faces to keep the gnats away, and then we was on our way again.

We went by Frish Fish Camp. They waved when we went by. We pushed on 'cause they was nothin' on the bank but trees. We got to where we should stick to the edge, but it were bad mud there and lots of sawgrass.

Byron sed, "They's a big gator!"

He were 'bout 12 feet long. I told Byron, "Some day we gonna kill 'im and skin 'im."

He went under and we didn't know where he were at. Then he come up again. He were goin' the other way. I'm shore glad. It'd be hard to kill 'im with a bamboo pole.

We finally got through the muddy places. We poled close to the bank. It were close to 1 o'clock. We may not make it back from Leesburg afore dark, but we was shore gonna try.

We went by Love Point. Betty Jean sed, "They call it Love Point 'cause that's where my boy friend goes to park when we're on a date."

The bottom were not mud now so we was makin' better time. I shore do wish Uncle Will could see us now. He'd say, "What y'all boys gonna do next? Lord 'o mercy, stay out of trouble!"

We could see Leesburg but we still had a ways to go. We passed 9th Street Canal. Then we was where them rich kids from school live. We pushed on by there to Monkey Island. We could see the dock. So we poled up to the dock and laid the pole on the float, tied it to the dock and walked down Dixie Avenue.

When we got to Highway 27 we stuck up our thumbs to catch a ride. A man and a woman wanted to know what we was doin'. We told them, "We made a raft and poled it to Leesburg from Okahumpka, but we was now tired and needed to git back home."

His wife asked us where the raft were and we told her we left it at the dock. They gived us a ride and let us out in Okahumpka. Betty Jean told Byron she had to get the bathin' suit off so her mama wouldn't know what she done.

So we stopped at the old Post Office. She taked it off. I went home and supper were ready. All I et all day were a candy bar and 2 cans of sardines. So I were hungry.

Mama had cooked up a big ole pot of lima beans and some corn-bread, and I hadda big glass of milk. After I et, I walked out on the porch where my dad were.

He sed, "How were the trip?" I jist telled 'im it were fun.

About 2 weeks later they had a picture of our float in the paper. They wanted to know where it come from. I knowed who left it there and I telled Byron, "I don't thank we should tell nobody. No tellin' what they'd do to us."

They put the raft on the bank and then they hauled it to the dump. But it shore were fun. Maybe we'll do that again!

Water Lilies   *Peg Urban*

These water lilies are locally called "Bonnets" or "Spatter-dock." They grow along rivers and lakesides. The bird who walks on them is a moor hen.

Peg Urban

The Hog Trap

Chapter 15

It were a Friday and we was tryin' to figure out what we was gonna do. I asked Byron if'n he wanted to spend the night in the swamp.

Byron sed, "Let's go build a hog trap. The man over on the creek has one and he can tell us how to build one." I shore wished Uncle Will was still here. He'd know how.

Saturday come 'round and we walked over to the creek and knocked on the door of that old shack. It really looked bad. But the man sed, "Come on in."

I warn't shore I wanted to go inside, but we done it anyway. It warn't that bad. At least it were clean. He'd jist had breakfast and he were cleanin' up the dishes. He asked if'n we'd like a cup of coffee.

We sed, "Shore." It were black and strong! I may not sleep for a week. Then we telled 'im we wanted to build a hog trap. He wanted to know if'n it were a big hog.

We sed, "It's as big as a calf and it has bad lookin' tusks, and it foams at the mouth."

Then he telled us, "When a boar hogs smells somebody, he foams at the mouth."

He telled us he'd help us build it for some of the pork, but he sed,

Skeeters and Hogs and Mules, Oh My!

"The big boar hogs would stink so bad y'all can't eat 'im. So y'all should start with a small hog."

He sed he had some wire, and we helped 'im load all the stuff in 'is wagon. He got 'is mule. He wanted to know what we was gonna use for bait.

I sed, "My dad'll give us some sweet feed."

We stopped by the house to git a bucket full of sweet feed, and went down the clay road and turned on Stage Coach Road. We went by Uncle Will's ole house. That man were there but he didn't wave. He jist looked at us.

We knowed where the hog trail were and where we thought we should set the trap. We built it and it looked real good. We agreed that the first hog we catched we'd give to that man who helped us, after we cleaned it.

So we set the trigger and put some sweet feed 'round the trigger. We headed home, went down Stage Coach Road and down the clay road. When we went by Uncle Will's ole house, that man jist looked at us 'gain.

Byron stayed at 'is house, and then I gived the man who helped us with the trap some feed for 'is mule.

That night I were happy 'bout our hog trap. I could jist see that hog in the trap.

Sunday mornin' we went to Sunday School. I didn't pay no 'tention to what were bein' sed. I were jist thinkin' 'bout our trap.

I rushed home and changed my clothes and got a bite to eat. My mama wanted to know what the hurry were. So I told 'er 'bout that hog trap. She jist sed to be careful and and warned me that some hogs is bad. I shore didn't tell 'er 'bout that big boar hog. That's the one we wanted to catch.

I got Lewis' gun and 'bout 6 shells. Then I stopped at Byron's and he got 'is gun. Betty Jean wanted to go, but Byron telled 'er she couldn't go 'cause we didn't know what we might have in the trap.

We waded 'cross the pond. When we went by Uncle Will's ole house, the man had a cleaned hog hangin' up. I looked at Byron and he sed, "I bet that's our hog we catched, and he done taked it."

We walked in the grove back in the woods where we had the hog pen. The trap were sprung and there were blood in the pen. We looked over by the water and there were the hog head and hide.

We shore was mad! But they were nothin' we could do. We didn't re-set the trap. We'd do it Friday when we got in from school. We walked back toward Byron's house and seen our hog hangin' along the way.

We walked over to the creek and told the man that lived there what had happened. He hooked the mule to the wagon, got 'is gun and sed, "Let's go, boys."

We rode down the clay road, turned up Stage Coach Road and turned in at Uncle Will's ole house. The man were cuttin' up the hog. The creek man got 'is gun and we walked 'round the house.

Sed, "I shoot hog thieves." And he raised 'is gun.

I thought shore he were gonna shoot 'im. The man begged 'im not to shoot 'im.

He sed, "I stole the hog. I didn't thank nobody would care."

The creek man sed, "I got a wash tub in the wagon back there. Jist put the meat in it. And if'n y'all give them boys any more trouble in them woods, I'll be back and I'll shoot y'all twice in the eyes and put y'all in a gator hole. Y'all hear what I'm sayin'? If'n y'all woulda asked we woulda gived y'all part of it. Now if'n y'all git an'thang else out of our trap y'all shore won't like what I'll do. "

We loaded the meat up and got back on the wagon. Then he telled us boys, "If'n he gives y'all boys a hard time, y'all jist let me know."

When we got back at Byron's house the man sed, "Git some pork to take with y'all."

But we telled 'im, "Y'all can have it all and we'll git some next time."

He sed, "Y'all boys shore 'bout that?

We sed, "Yes. We're shore."

Then he sed, "I knowed y'all boys would do what ever'body 'round here has sed 'bout y'all."

Then he dropped me off at my house. My dad stepped out and spoke to 'im. He handed my dad a backstrap and sed, "Cook this up for that boy."

I asked my mama if'n I could give that man a pan of cracklin' corn-bread. I knowed he'd like it.

I got ready for church. Byron were settin' on the steps and sed, "We need to string Uncle Will's house where that man lives 'gain one day."

Skeeters and Hogs and Mules, Oh My!

I sed, "We will, one day."

We left church and when I got home it were late. My brother had already laid down. If'n it were cold I'd a-put my cold feet on 'im.

The weekend shore passed fast.

Cracklin' Cornbread

½ c water ground cornmeal
2 Tbsp Sugar
3 Tbsp lard
½ c flour
1 egg
Milk enough to mix
1 c cracklin'
On hog killin' day, cook all the lard out of the hog skin.
Then squeeze out all the lard you can
Dry in the sun
Take a flour sack and put the skin in the sack
Beat it with a hammer till it's broke in small pieces
Mix with the cornbread
Bake for 20 minutes at 350 degrees

The Night in
Lake Dunham Swamp
Chapter 16

It were a short week. We knowed what we was gonna do on the weekend. We was gonna set the trap 'gain and spend the night on the platform.

We'd take a blanket 'cause it can git cold. We made us a piece of screen wire to keep the skeeters off. I thought, *Shore hope it works.*

When school were out on Friday we didn't ride the bus home. We went to the A&P Store in Leesburg and asked Mr. Scott if'n we could have some bad fruit. He gived us all we could carry. We walked down to Highway 27 and catched a ride real quick. We didn't beat the bus, but we come close.

We dropped the bag at Byron's house. I went home and changed clothes, got me a long sleeved shirt, my hat, Lewis' gun, and 10 shells. I told my mama I were gonna kill a hog . She sed to be shore to shoot it in the head so we didn't ruin the meat.

I got to Byron's. He were ready to go. Then Betty Jean wanted to go with us. I didn't really care, but it might be a bad night. We did need 'er to help carry some of our stuff.

We got to the platform. We knowed we had to git ever'thang done afore dark. Byron and Betty Jean set the hog trap. He kept some of the good fruit so we could eat it.

The screen worked out good. We put some of the rest of the fruit in a flour sack and pulled it up the tree. We needed our guns up there too. We wouldn't leave 'em on the ground again like we done afore. We unloaded 'em and then climbed the tree.

It were gittin' dark. The screen wire shore helped. We had the blanket. I shore hoped it wouldn't rain. The night looked good right then. I thought it were gonna be fun. We laid there and talked 'bout the trap.

Betty Jean asked us if'n we was scared. We sed, "No".

She sed she liked it up there. We quit talkin' then. They's every kind of noise in this here swamp. And we went to sleep.

I don't know what time it were, but Betty Jean screamed. We all waked up. That big cat were on the platform with us! I seen 'is eyes. I grabbed my gun and pulled the trigger, but it jist clicked. I'd forgotten to put a shell in it! I found the shell and loaded up, but by then the cat were gone!

I never thought 'bout a cat climbin' the tree with us, but he shore did. I guess he woulda ate good with 3 of us there. If'n Betty Jean hadn't a screamed, no tellin' what woulda happened. I were shore glad we brought 'er along. She sed that cat licked 'er foot, but I don't thank so.

After that Betty Jean wanted to go home, but we told her she'd have to wait 'til daylight afore we could go. I rolled over and went back to sleep. Then Byron shook Betty Jean and she shook me. They were a noise over where the trap were. It sounded like somebody were tearin' down a house.

Then it got quiet. Byron sed that whatever were there were gone now. Y'all could hear all kind of other noise. Then the noise over where the trap were started up again.

Betty Jean wanted to know if'n we was gonna go over there. But we told her, "Not in the dark!"

It got a little chilly. We went back to sleep but we knowed she were awake 'cause she'd give us a punch if'n somethang made too much noise. It warn't quiet, but at least that loud noise were gone.

The sun were comin' up. It had been a long night, but I slept most of it. We opened the bag and et some of the stuff in the bag. Byron sed, "I thank we can climb down now."

I looked all 'round on the ground but didn't see nothin'. We climbed down. Them skeeters was shore rough.

We waded out on the log, but I made shore I had a shell in my gun and Byron checked 'is gun too.

When we come out at the grove they were that big hog track. I shore hope we'd catched 'im in the trap. We walked to where the trap were at, but there warn't no hog in there. The hog had done tore up our trap. He had a hard time doin' it, but he got out.

The ground shore were tore up. I'd like to have kilt 'im. But in a way, I'm glad I didn't.

We climbed back up on the platform and got our blanket and looked at the tree. You could see where the cat climbed up the tree. We taked all the stuff back over to the tree house. Then Byron sed, "Let's go take a bath."

I thought that sounded like a good idea. So we walked over to the spring, stripped off all our clothes, got some sand and washed up and rinsed off. All 3 of us felt better and we put our clothes back on and started walkin' back.

We seen the hog, but he were too far away to shoot 'im. So that's for another day.

We stopped by Byron's house and he told Betty Jean to not tell nobody 'bout that big cat. I went on home and taked a real bath. That night I et supper and fell asleep. My bed shore felt good!

The next mornin' I got up and went to church. When I got there Betty Jean telled Byron she didn't thank she'd do that again.

Skeeters and Hogs and Mules, Oh My!

Florida Cat

The Wagon

Chapter 17

School were not real bad, and this week were a short one, so I asked Byron if'n he wanted to go over on the creek and tell that man what the hog had did to the trap. So on Friday, when we got out of school, we walked over to 'is house on the creek.

He were settin' outside. He told us he were sick. Then we told 'im what the hog had did to the trap.

He told us how to fix it. "Put the post on the outside. Put more posts on the inside. And put the posts deeper than what y'all had afore."

Then we told 'im 'bout the big cat. He jist looked at us. He sed, "I thank it'd be best if'n y'all stayed out of that swamp."

That's what ever'body keeps tellin' us. Then he told us we could use 'is mule and wagon to haul the posts. So we told 'im we'd do it on Saturday.

Saturday mornin' we walked over to the creek. He warn't outside so we knocked on the door. He jist hollered to come in.

We walked inside. He looked real bad. I asked 'im if'n he'd like to go to the doctor, but he sed he didn't. He asked if'n we'd take the chickens home with us. And he didn't feel like feedin' the pigs neither. We asked if'n we could take the mule and feed 'im and if'n we could used the wagon.

He sed, "Shore."

We loaded up some posts and caught the chickens, then tied they's legs. Then we catched the pigs and tied they's legs too. They didn't like that at all. But we loaded 'em on the wagon. We got what feed he had and loaded it up.

Byron sed he'd take the mule home with 'im. He had a place to put 'im.

Afore we put the pigs in the pen, we caught the boar hog. They didn't none of them like that. We put screw worm medicine on them and put the chickens in with mama's chickens, but not the rooster. One rooster would kill the other. So we turned 'im loose in the yard.

We taked the posts over to the hog trap and we worked on the hog trap 'bout all day. When we left it were in real good shape.

We put the mule in the field at Byron's house and gived 'im some feed and rubbed 'im down. He liked that.

I asked Byron if'n he were gonna ride 'im to church. We both laffed. Then I told Byron, "We is mule skinners jist like them people used to be."

Then Byron sed, "I bet afore it's over that mule skins both of us."

He were a good mule. We'll keep 'im 'til the man gits well. He shore does like to be rubbed down.

I walked across the field and my mama asked me where them chickens come from. Then I told 'her 'bout the man on the creek bein' sick and he couldn't take care of them. And that we had 'is pigs too.

When my dad come home from work I told 'im 'bout the sick man. He wanted to go see 'im.

So we went to 'is house and knocked on the door. He jist told us to come in like afore. He shore did look real bad.

My dad asked if'n he wanted to see a doctor, but he didn't. We left and on the way back my dad sed, "He's dyin', and I thank he wants to."

We got up Sunday mornin' and put on our good clothes and went to church. After church I come home and taked some food over to the man on the creek. He warn't there. I didn't know what to thank.

I walked back home, and put the food on the table. I told my mama he warn't home. I shore would like to know what happened to 'im.

I got up Monday mornin' and went to school. I told Byron what I'd done so when we got off the bus we walked over to 'is house on the creek. We knocked on the door, but they warn't no answer. So we opened the door and looked inside. He jist warn't there.

We left and started to walk back home. I felt sad. I jist knowed somethang were wrong.

A man from down the road walked up and told us the sick man died the day afore. He left a note that sed, "Have my ashes placed in the creek and give ever'thang I got to them two young boys." He didn't own the house, but the man told us to go back in and take anythang we wanted.

Well, he didn't have hardly nothin'. We got a fry pan. He had a gun, but somebody had done got it. I telled the man, "I hope we can keep the mule."

He sed, "Shore. Go git the plow and all the farm equipment too."

So we walked back home to git the wagon, hitched the mule and went back to the creek. We loaded the wagon with all the farm stuff. We had a wagon full. I looked inside the house again. We shore didn't need nothin' there. We didn't have much, but he had even less.

I wish we'd asked 'im what is name were. They asked if'n we could put 'is ashes in the creek, and we telled them we could do it. So a neighbor handed us a box. It shore warn't very much. I wondered where the rest of it were.

We walked down to the creek, opened the box and poured the ashes out. The wind blowed them all over us, but most of it went in the creek.

Byron sed, "He shore were good to us." I jist wanted to cry.

We done heerd 'im call the mule "Charley", so that's what we called 'im.

We was ridin' 'cross the field with Charley, and Byron telled me to hang on to the reins 'cause he needed to git a stick and kill a big ole rattlesnake.

He got back on the wagon and sed, "That snake didn't rattle at all."

I sed, "Maybe he were sick."

Byron sed, "Well, he's dead now."

We went back to Byron's house, unloaded the farm equipment and put it under the shed to keep it outta the rain. Then we put Charley in the barn and gived 'im some feed and rubbed 'im down like my dad telled me to do. Then Charley rolled in the dirt! I guess that keeps the bugs off 'im.

Skeeters and Hogs and Mules, Oh My!

I were happy to git the farm stuff, but I shore hated to see that man die. We seen the wheel on the wagon had a bad spot. So we pulled the wagon wheel off and taked it to my dad to fix. The wagon had some bad boards, so we went to git some lumber where they tored the house down over on the curve, and fixed the broken stuff.

A mule skinner is a mule driver.

A working mule, name of Charley.

Miss Sweetie Pie

Chapter 18

When we got on the school bus, Byron told me a man come by 'is house and wanted us to plow 'is field so's he could have a big garden over by the creek. He sed he'd pay us 8 dollars to plow and plant it.

So when we got off the bus on Friday, we put the plow, the planter and drag in the wagon. My dad gived me the mower he had and we tied it on the back of the wagon. Then we got the eye hoe and yard rake. I told my mama what we was gonna do. She fixed us a lunch. She knowed Byron liked sweet taters. I thank if'n he had a choice of ice cream or sweet taters he'd take the sweet taters. So she put lots of sweet taters in our lunch.

Come Saturday mornin' we was ready to go at day light. It taked us 'bout an hour to git to 'is house. When we got there he were jist gittin' up. He shore were a big ole man. He done et a whole bunch of good food to git that big. His wife come to the door. She were good lookin' and she smelled good too. She had on some good smellin' stuff.

He told us 'is name were Mike. That were easy to 'member, and he told us 'is wife's name were Sweetie Pie. He told us she made the best banana cream pies you ever et. Sed he could eat a bunch of them.

He showed us where the garden were and we hooked up Charley to the mower. We made for the spot where he wanted the garden. Goodness! That grass were 'bout knee high. We mowed a big spot. Then we raked the hay and made a big hay stack for Charley, and we started to hook up the plow.

Miss Sweetie Pie called out and sed it were time to eat breakfast. We was barefooted and the dirt were on our feet, but she sed we could wash our feet and dry them off.

We walked inside. Mr. Mike had 'is fork and knife all ready to eat. She had pancakes and store-bought s'rup with 2 pancakes for ever'body, and bread with store-bought butter on it. She made us hot chocolate with somethin' on the top. It shore were good. We knowed they warn't from Okahumpka.

We thanked 'er for the breakfast. It were real good, but woulda been better if'n we had some grits. They say people from up north don't eat grits.

We went back out and hooked up Charley. Byron were plowin' and I were pickin' up trash and weeds. It were 'bout noon and the field were plowed. Byron hooked up the drag to make it smooth. It were lookin' real good.

Mr. Mike come outside and sed lunch were ready, but we telled 'im we bringed our own lunch. He telled us to wash our feet and face and hands and come on inside and eat. Well, we warn't gonna miss out on a good lunch.

He were belly-up to the table and were ready to eat. Miss Sweetie Pie done cooked some stuff, but I didn't know what it were. It were real good. We finished lunch and she gived us both a big piece of banana cream pie. Now I knowed why Mr. Mike were so big.

We set on the porch with Mr. Mike and Miss Sweetie Pie. She were a good cook and we shore did like 'er. She sed Mr. Mike needed to rake the front yard.

He whined 'bout it but he got the rake out. He didn't do a very good job though. We got the planter off the wagon and planted 3 rows of peas, then 4 rows of corn. We had to cut up poles and bedded up 3 rows of taters with a hoe. I planted them. Then we planted squash. Boy! This were gonna be a big garden. We planted some greens too.

I telled Byron I wondered who were gonna pick this garden. That big fat man warn't gonna do it. We planted all he wanted planted.

We kept hearin' somebody shootin' over by Clear Water Lake. We asked Mr. Mike 'bout it, and he sed they's a man over there that shoots 'is gun ever' Saturday.

We hooked up the pump in the creek and got it runnin'. It shore were doin' a good job and we was ready to leave. It were almost dark.

We told Mr. Mike we was gonna go and we thanked Miss Sweetie Pie for the meals. Mr. Mike paid us, but he gived each of us jist 1 dollar.

Byron sed, "Y'all told us 8 dollars."

But he sed, "That's too much money." And he walked back to the house.

We taked the 2 dollars and nailed 'em to the fence post. We was mad! But we did have a real good lunch.

I told Byron, "Let's plow it all up!"

We talked it over. Somebody's gonna have to keep the weeds out. We'd make 'im pay a high price to do it, but we'd git our money first.

We loaded up all our tools and left. I got home 'bout dark. My dad asked how our day went.

I told 'im, "Not good." Then I told 'im what that man done.

Time rolled 'round and in 'bout 2 weeks Miss Sweetie Pie stopped by Byron's and wanted us to plow the rows to git the weeds out of the garden.

But Byron told her how Mr. Mike paid us and we didn't wanna work for 'im no more.

Miss Sweetie Pie sed, "I'll pay y'all, but don't tell 'im." And she gived Byron 20 dollars so we'd weed the garden.

On Saturday Byron plowed out the middle while I used the hoe 'round the plants. It shore looks good.

We could still hear shootin' over by Clear Water Lake. We got most of the weeds out of the garden while Mr. Mike set on the porch. He shore don't look happy. Miss Sweetie Pie come out where we was workin' and told us she made a banana cream pie. She sed, "Mr. Mike thanks he's a gonna eat it, but I'm gonna give it to y'all boys and don't y'all let 'im have any of it."

Pretty soon she bringed out the pie with 2 forks. He seen what she had and jist knowed he were gonna git some of that pie. He watched

Skeeters and Hogs and Mules, Oh My!

Byron and me eat all but jist 1 piece of pie. It were a big piece, too. I telled Byron to give it to Charley.

We laffed. Mr. Mike were shore lookin' at it. Byron walked to where Charley were. Charley stuck 'is nose in the pie and gobbled it right up.

I looked at Mr. Mike and I jist knowed he wanted that big piece of pie. Then I heerd Miss Sweetie Pie tell 'im to settle up with us or they woundn't be no more banana cream pie 'round there.

He walked over to us and sed, "Boys, I done y'all wrong. Here's 30 dollars, if'n that's enough. I ain't had no pie in a long time and I know I done y'all wrong. I won't do it 'gain."

We thanked 'im. And ole Charley shore did like that pie.

Banana Cream Pie

The SUCKER

Chapter 19

This week were short and on Friday we talked it over and decided we'd go over to the swamp.

Then I telled Byron, "Let's go where they was shootin' them guns Saturday."

So we hitched up ole Charley. He shore were an old mule. He were slow, but he were better'n walkin'. We went by Snell Dairy, crossed the paved road and went through the woods. Charley done better on the sand road. I'd gotten my dad to trim Charley's feet so that helped 'im.

We seen the gun range and the grass were 'bout knee deep. We had the mower on the back of the wagon and I thought, *Maybe we could mow it.*

We rode Charley out there. Good thang Charley warn't 'fraid of them guns.

I asked Byron if'n he brought 'is gun. He sed, "Shore did."

They was shootin' 'bout 50 yards. Some was good and some was bad. The man that owned the shootin' range were in the Army. They sed he were a Full Bird Colonel and he were one of the best shots. They was shootin' for money.

They put a piece of paper over a washer and shot the middle out.

Skeeters and Hogs and Mules, Oh My!

I asked Byron if'n he could shoot out that-there hole, and he sed he could. I telled 'im I were gonna bet that man that he couldn't beat y'all. And if'n he beat y'all, we'd mow 'is grass where the shootin' range were. But if'n y'all beat 'im, we'd git 5 dollars.

Then I telled Byron, "I want y'all to miss one shot. Shoot to the side. We can sucker 'im in and we'll git 2 new guns out of the deal.

They was some good shooters, but Mr. Keith were real good. He shot a M1 Garand like in the Army. They sed he were a Green Beret. I don't know what that were but it must be real good.

They sold beer and cold drinks and hot dogs. We bringed a sweet tater with us and a water jug, and we bringed some sweet feed for Charley. He were a good ole mule. I wondered what he'd look like if'n he were green. I jist laffed inside.

After tellin' Mr. Keith 'bout the bet, he thought that would be a pretty good deal. Well, jist 'bout everyone heerd what were goin' on. I looked over and there stood the man that we went to Ocala with. He jist smiled. He knowed what we was doin'.

Byron got 'is .45-70 and 'is box of shells. The man shot first. He missed the first shot. Then he shot right through the center of that washer.

Mr. Keith thought that were pretty good, but not good enough.

Then Byron shot 5 times. He jist knicked the washer. So the man won.

I telled Byron I'd go hitch up the mower and mow the field. It didn't take long. Then we raked it up and put it on the wagon.

Mr. Keith sed that Byron were a good shot, but not good enough. He also sed we done a real good job in the grass, and wanted us to keep it mowed.

So I telled Mr. Keith we should shoot 'gain, and if'n we lose we would keep it mowed for a year. But if'n we won, he'd buy us both a new .22 mag Henry Rifle.

Mr. Keith sed, "Y'all boys know y'all are gonna lose."

I looked over at the man from the Ocala trip we taked, and he were jist a-smilin'. He knowed what we was gonna do.

Ever'one were waitin'. Then Mr. Keith sed, "Okay. That's a deal. Here's what we'll do. We'll both shoot 'til one misses. Is that okay?"

Byron sed, "Shore is."

Mr. Keith telled Byron he could shoot first. The man from the Ocala trip sed, "Anyone want a bet on the boys?"

I don't know how much he bet, but it were a pile of money.

Byron shot dead center. Then Mr. Keith shot dead center.

Then Byron shot dead center and Mr. Keith shot dead center.

Mr. Keith were good. After 'bout 4 times I were beginin' to thank I'd be mowin' all summer. Then Byron shot dead center and Mr. Keith shot and the washer flew in the air. I seen the man from the Ocala trip start to pick up the money.

Mr. Keith sed, "Y'all won, but let me win with 'nother shot."

I telled 'im, "We shoot one rifle for 4 cases of .22 mag shells."

He sed he would do that.

We looked at the man. He jist smiled. They got ready to shoot. The man were bettin' on Byron, but he didn't have as many people that wanted to gamble.

Byron shot dead center. Mr. Keith shot dead center.

Then Mr. Keith moved them 75 yards. Byron sed it were okay.

Byron shot dead center. Mr. Keith shot but missed it and telled Byron, "Y'all won fair and square. I do what I say I'll do. Next Saturday we'll have a turkey shoot. I'll have y'all's guns and shells then. I have 2 friends who think they's the best. I'd like for y'all come and shoot again."

The week went by fast. We got the man from Ocala to pay our dollar to shoot the turkey and bought 3 chances.

When we got there, the first thang they sed were, "Them boys can't shoot."

But Mr. Keith telled 'em, "They already paid, so they can shoot."

They sed, "No turkey call, and no loud noise, then."

So we went up there and here come the turkey. Byron knocked 'is head off. He shot 3 times and kilt 3 turkeys.

At lunch time the man from Ocala bought our lunch. He bought us a hot dog and a pink soda water. After lunch they all lined up to shoot 'gain. Mr. Keith telled Byron he could shoot last. He didn't want them to know how good he were.

After ever'one had shot, Mr. Keith telled one of them men he'd like to shoot for money. I seen a smile come on 'is face. He jist knowed he were gonna win.

They wanted to know what they were gonna shoot for, and Mr. Keith told them, "Gun for gun."

I shore hoped Byron wouldn't miss.

They flipped a coin to see who'd go first. Byron shot second, which were all right with Byron. They each shot 4 times. Nobody missed. Then they moved 75 yards. I seen the man sweatin' a little bit. They each shot 5 times more and nobody missed.

The man knowed thang's warn't goin' 'is way.

So they moved it to 80 yards. The man shot and he missed. Mr. Keith sed, "Byron y'all shoot and if'n y'all don't miss y'all won."

Byron put in a shell and fired. They warn't no sound. The man told Byron, "I knowed y'all hit it dead center. I don't even have to look."

Mr. Keith walked over to the man and the man started to hand over 'is gun, but Mr. Keith told 'im to jist keep it. He sed, "Y'all was set up jist like them boys done me."

Then Mr. Keith turned to the us and sed, "Boys, I'll have y'all's guns next week."

I told Byron, "He don't have to give us them guns. Let's do like he done. It'll be more fun that way. "

So we sed, "Mr. Keith, we don't want the guns and shells."

I seen a tear in 'is eye.

Then a man we didn't even know told us to not leave. Sed he'd be right back.

He were gone 'bout an hour, so Mr. Keith told us we could have us 'nother hot dog.

The man Byron shot against asked 'im, "Who teached y'all how to shoot?"

Byron jist told 'im he were born shootin' and the gun he were shootin' with belonged to 'is Uncle Kucher.

When the man got back after 'bout an hour, he were carryin' a gold-cored .22 mag. He gived both Byron and me one. And he gived us each a case of bullets. He sed, "Y'all boys are jist good boys."

He didn't even know us.

Then Mr. Keith asked Byron, "Did y'all really miss when y'all shot on the mowin' job?"

Byron grinned and sed, "Ask Red over there."

Then he sed, "Boys, y'all can shoot here any time y'all want to."

Then he sed, "Would y'all keep the range mowed?"

We sed, "We shore would."

In real life Mr. Keith were a Full Bird Colonel Green Beret Ranger. I'm shore he seen some real bad stuff.

Red Fussel

BILL AND LARRY

Chapter 20

What I'm 'bout to tell y'all were telled to me by Judy. I shore believed what Judy telled me 'bout what Bill and Larry done.

Them boys lived over on Turkey Lake. They's big ole boys. They's mama sed that when they set down to eat what she cooked, they et it all. They even licked the pot clean!

They's a man, he lives over by Twin Lake. He has chickens and hogs and goats. He started to notice 'is eggs was missin'—'bout a dozen a week. Then it got to be a dozen a day. He come to Okahumpka and asked Byron if'n we was stealin' 'is eggs.

We telled 'im, "No, and that a be too far for us to go, anyhow."

Then he started missin' 'is chickens. Not many, but he were gonna catch who were doin' it.

Well, the real thieves' mama wondered where they got the eggs and chickens. They telled 'er they was pullin' moss to make money to buy them chickens and a new hog.

The sheriff come to Okahumpka and asked us if'n we was stealin' them chickens and eggs and a hog, too. We telled 'im we didn't do it, but I don't thank he believed us. I shore would hate to go to jail for somethang somebody else done.

One night the man that owned them chickens seen one of them boys sneak by 'is chicken pen. He got 'is shot gun, slipped out by the barn and stuck that there gun in Bill's side. Bill stuck 'is hands in the air.

That man were mad at Bill, and Bill cried. He shore hoped he wouldn't shoot 'im. Well, the man knowed them boys and telled Larry to come on out. He sed, "Come on out Larry. I know y'all's out there."

Larry walked out with 'is hands in the air. They knowed they was in real trouble. Larry whispered, "Bill, y'all thank if'n we run he'd shoot us?"

Bill jist looked at 'im and sed, "Y'all can run if'n y'all want to, but I'm not."

The man got in 'is truck and telled the boys to climb in the back.

Larry telled Bill, "We can run now."

But Bill sed, "I'm more scared what our mama's gonna do than what he's gonna do."

It were 'bout 9 o'clock when they drived up to they's house. The man blowed 'is horn and the boys' daddy come out. The man telled 'im what the boys had did.

The boys didn't say a word. They knowed they was in trouble. Then the man left. They met the mother at the door. She jist pointed to the bedroom.

They took off they's clothes and went to bed. They couldn't go to sleep 'cause they jist knowed they's mama were gonna beat them to death. It shore were a long night.

Next mornin' they come to the table and she were cookin' some of them eggs they stole. Larry telled Bill, "Them eggs don't even taste good."

They's mama still hadn't sed nothin' to them. They jist wished she would holler at 'em or somethang. They was 'fraid she'd put stripes on they's backside.

They et their breakfast and started out the door, when she stopped them. She telled them to go git they's eye hoe and go over there and hoe that man's orange grove. She telled them if'n they warn't workin' when she come by, she'd call the sheriff and have 'im put them in jail.

The boys didn't say a word. They knowed when she sed somethang that it would be did.

They worked till noon and didn't have no lunch, so they et some oranges. Some fried chicken woulda tasted good. They worked 'til 'bout dark and then walked home. They's mama had supper fixed and they had a real good meal. They took a bath, went to bed and hoped they didn't have to go back and hoe them oranges trees 'gain the next day.

When the sun come up they's mama told them to git up. She had breakfast ready. She had cooked the last of the eggs they stole. She told them to git they's hoes and go back to the grove with no lunch.

Bill told Larry, "I guess we eat oranges 'gain."

It were 'bout 11:45 and the man that owned the grove drived up. He had a cooler with some drinks in it and a box of fried chicken. He didn't say nothin'. He jist set it out. So the boys stopped for lunch. They et their lunch and drinked all them drinks. They shore would like to go home but they knowed they's mama would tell them when they could stop.

It shore were hot in the grove. Bill sed, "If'n we had to do it all over, we shore wouldna did it, but it were fun when we was doin' it."

They worked in the grove all week, day light 'til dark. They had one row of trees left. Then they seen they's mama comin' down the road. They didn't know what she were gonna have them do. And the man who owned the oranges were comin' down the road too. That didn't look good.

Larry told Bill, "I don't like what's gonna happen now. Maybe we oughtta run!"

Bill sed, "Where y'all gonna run to?"

The man got out of 'is truck and they leaned they's hoes against a tree. They's mama told them, "When y'all finish that there last row y'all can quit, but this here man has somethang to tell y'all boys."

He sed, "Boys, I were mad as I could be when y'all stole my chickens and eggs and hog. I got the hog back and y'all et the chickens and the eggs. I figured up y'all's pay for weedin' the oranges, but y'all's mama sed y'all et up y'all's pay. Y'all done a good job here. The trees look real good. How 'bout we jist call it even? I ain't mad now, and if'n I need help I'll let y'all know. But no more stealin'."

With that he walked over and got in 'is truck and left. We got our hoes and started weedin'. They's mama told them to do the last row.

It were real hot but they knowed they's still have to walk home. She left and they got home 'bout dark.

Bill telled Larry, "I shore ain't stealin' no more chickens!"

MISS SANDERS

Chapter 21

I were feedin' the hogs out by the barn. We cooked most of the food we gived them hogs.

My dad come out and sed, "What y'all need to do is go to Miss Sanders on the grove. She needs 'er cane patch weeded. Go to Byron's and git the mule and y'all and Byron go cultivate the middle of the grove. Then clean the hoe as good as y'all can. But don't charge 'er. She don't got nobody to help 'er."

I told Byron what my dad sed. Byron sed we could do it on Saturday.

We loaded the wagon with what we thought we needed to git rid of them weeds. She lived on the old Knight place. Byron's grandpa lived there a long time ago. When we got there we undone the cultivator. Byron hitched it to Charley and I took the eye hoe.

We was in the cane patch when Miss Sanders walked out on the porch. I never seen 'er afore. She had a gun on 'er side. Y'all could tell she dipped snuff.

She had on boots like a man. She sed, "What y'all boys doin' in my cane patch?"

We telled 'er we was cleanin' the grass out so the cane could grow better. She telled us she couldn't pay us. But then we telled 'er we wasn't gonna charge nothin'.

We seen 'er spit so we really knowed she were a dippin' snuff. I asked, "Byron, y'all want a dip?"

He sed, "No, I done dipped one time with RH. That were enough."

It were 'bout noon and we had it all did. It started to rain, so we taked Charley inside the barn. They was a buggy and a whole bunch of farm equipment and a wagon like the one Byron had. Miss Sanders called us to the house so we left Charley in the barn. We gived 'im some hay and some water so he were happy.

We was standin' on the porch and she asked if'n we'd go to Mr. Hall's store and git 'er some stuff. She'd made out a list for us. I telled Byron she bought Butter Cup snuff. That's what most people used. I didn't look at the rest of the stuff on the list.

It had jist 'bout quit rainin'. Charley wouldn't mind a jist little rain.

We got to Mr. Hall's store. He put what Miss Sanders wanted in a bag and handed it to us, and he handed us 'nother bag with a Black Cow candy bar in it. We telled 'im to take it off 'er bill 'cause she didn't have no money for it. But he sed he didn't charge 'er for it.

We thanked 'im for the Black Cow candy bar.

So we et it for lunch. We got back at 'er shack. That's all it were. We lived in a rundown house, but she lived in a worse one. It were jist a shack.

Then I asked Miss Sanders if'n she could shoot that gun there on 'er side. She telled us to set up 5 cans on 'er fence. It were mistin' rain and Charley were in the barn and we was on the porch. She grabbed 'er pistol and fired 5 times. All 5 cans was gone.

We asked 'er why she wore that-there gun and she sed, "They's a big ole cat out there. I seen 'im sometimes. He never gived me no trouble or I woulda kilt 'im."

I thought, I *bet it were that same cat we seen.*

I telled Byron that the next time we go over to where they shoot, we should take 'er with us.

We telled 'er we had to leave and she thanked us. We was tired but we'd done a good deed for the day. We left.

We put Charley in the shed and gived 'im some feed and rubbed 'im down. He liked that. I guess ever'body likes to be rubbed.

Skeeters and Hogs and Mules, Oh My!

I walked 'cross the field, taked my Saturday bath, et supper, laid down in my bed and went right to sleep. I never even knowed when my brother come home.

We went to school the next week. It were the last of October and y'all could tell winter were acomin' on.

My dad telled me, "Y'all need to bank Miss Sander's cane so it won't freeze."

So I telled 'im I'd git Byron and we'd do it on Saturday.

We asked that red-headed girl that lives on Red Hill Grove to help us with the cane. I already done banked our cane, so I knowed how to do it.

Come Saturday we hooked up the wagon and picked up that red-headed girl down the road and 'er friend. She telled us that her boyfriend telled 'er to tell us not to mess with 'er or he would knock us in the side of the head!

I didn't pay no attention to that. He couldn't whip both of us. She shore were good lookin'. She brought a friend with 'er too.

My dad made some sharp boards to take the tassels off, so we let the girls do that and Byron and me cut the cane. We'd cut the cane and put it in a pile. Then we'd cut another row. My dad stopped by and telled us to take the cane to the mill. So we loaded the wagon 'til it were full.

It were 'bout 11 when we had all the wagon would hold. Byron and the red-headed girl and 'er friend left for the cane mill. Miss Sanders gived me a pair of gloves and a bucket to git 'er some stingin' nettles. She needed a whole bucket full. I shore didn't know what for. Them thangs sting to even touch.

Out behind 'er house were a big patch of it. I taked my knife and cut them nettles 'til I had a bucket full. Then she telled me to cut them leaves off. She sent me back for more leaves. I got 'nother whole bucket full.

She had a cast iron pot on the stove. She taked some fatback grease and pored it on the leaves in the pot. She made some cornbread and telled me to go git some more leaves. She had a small pot and she put them leaves in it. She boiled them and jist let 'em set.

Byron were comin' down the road with that red-headed girl and 'er friend. Miss Sanders telled us to wash up.

Now, I never et no stingin' nettle afore. If'n they sting y'all's belly what y'all gonna do? So I thought I'd let them eat them first. If'n they hollered, I wouldn't eat it.

She set the iron pot on two bricks on the table. She looked at our hands afore she let us eat. Then she put a good helpin' on all our plates.

I set there and watched Byron eat. He sed, "It shore is good."

I were waitin' for 'im to start screamin', but he wanted 'nother helpin'. So I et mine. It were real good. Miss Sanders didn't have no ice but we had tea with sugar in it.

We finished lunch and went back to the cane. The girls told Miss Sanders they'd help 'er in the kitchen. But she told 'em to go back to cuttin' cane.

We hauled 4 loads to the mill and had one load to go. My dad had an old tarp so we put the tarp over the cane so it wouldn't freeze, and then we taked the red-head girl and 'er friend back to Red Hill Grove.

Well, guess who were at 'er house when we taked 'er home. Her boyfriend! He balled up 'is fist and shook it at us. We jist turned the wagon 'round and headed back home.

We got back to Byron's house and put Charley in the barn and rubbed 'im down.

I walked 'cross the field, went into my house, and filled my tub with water. I needed a bath! Then I put the tub by the fireplace, taked off my clothes and crawled in the tub. I touched my rear end on that-there hot tub. Thank I musta burnt a streak on my behind, but I still taked my bath. Then I crawled in bed. I were tired.

The next thang I knowed it were daylight. I looked over and Lewis warn't in bed. My mama told me Lewis had went to Tampa.

Well, I looked outside and seen a heavy frost. If we hadn't a-banked Miss Sander's cane yesterday, it wouldn't be no good today.

My dad sed he were gonna make s'rup outta Miss Sander's cane on Saturday and to ask Byron if'n we could use the mule.

Of course, Byron sed, "Shore."

So Saturday rolled 'round and Byron picked up them two girls that helped with the cane. The red-headed girl's boyfriend shook 'is fist at Byron.

I told Byron, "Maybe I should whip 'im!"

Skeeters and Hogs and Mules, Oh My!

We rode over to the cane mill, hitched up Charley, but he jist stood there. My dad sed, "Go git the feed bucket."

So then Charley walked 'round and 'round and 'round tryin' to reach that feed bucket. We fed the cane at the mill and juice flowed in the wooden barrel. When it were full they put it in a big ole steel pot.

It come to a boil real quick. It were real hot. They fired it with lighter knots. Ole Charley were still goin' 'round and 'round and 'round. We done squeezed 'nother barrel. Ever once in a while they put a drop of the s'rup in cold water. That's how then knowed it were ready.

Then they skimmed the top to git the trash off. When it were ready, they funneled it into them whiskey bottles that come from the Cane Patch Beer Joint. It shore looked good.

Miss Sanders come outside and telled my dad that he shore knowed how to make good s'rup.

Then they put the last barrel of juice in the kettle, skimmed the top and cooked it 'til it were jist right. Ole Charley stopped and we gived 'im some sweet feed. My! My! He shore did like that.

The last itty bit my dad boiled 'til it were real thick. He dipped it up and put it on a piece of tin. When it cooled he gived it to us kids. We twisted it and pulled it 'til we got most of the s'rup out. Then we taked a hammer and hit it 'til it broke in a bunch of pieces. We all got some. It were real stickey but it shore were good. The day had been fun.

We taked an orange box and put the s'rup bottles in the box and taked it to Miss Sanders. She tried to git my dad to take part of it but he telled Miss Sanders to give the girls some s'rup for helpin'. So she gived both girls a bottle of s'rup and then she kissed them. They thanked 'er.

When we got it all did she even kissed Byron and me. We asked Miss Sanders if'n she'd like to go where they was shootin' next Saturday. She sed that she shore would.

We taked the red-headed girl and her friend home and there stood her boy friend! I heerd her friend say, "I shore wish he would jist leave!"

We left and made it back to Byron's house, put Charley in the barn, gived 'im some hay and water and rubbed 'im down. It had been a long day, but a good one.

I walked home and taked my bath. I thought I shoulda laid on my brother's side of the bed afore I taked my bath to make it sticky from the cane juice, but my mama wouldn't like that a bit.

The week passed quick. Them city folk jist don't know how to have fun! I'd like to go to the picture show like they do, but I wouldn't change that for what we do.

We hooked up Charley to the wagon Friday afternoon and rode to Miss Sanders house, knocked on the door, and out stepped a big ole boy. We told 'im we wanted to see Miss Sanders, and he wanted to know what for. She come out and telled 'im to git back in the house. We asked 'er if'n she'd like to go over to the gun range in the mornin'.

She sed, "Shore."

We picked 'er up in the wagon 'bout 7 and went by the Sneel Dairy and through the woods. We had the mower on the back and telled Miss Sanders we needed to mow the gun range. She got down and helped us rake it clean. We put the hay in the wagon for Charley.

Out walked Mr. Keith He sed it looked real good and he wanted to pay us to mow it. We telled 'im we wouldn't take no money but if'n 'is wife had somethang to eat we'd eat it. So he asked 'is wife to cook some more grits and eggs. We et 'er good breakfast. Miss Sanders said she didn't wanna eat, but she wanted to know if'n that lady were our mama. He telled 'er we that we was jist friends.

We set on the porch and talked 'bout all kind of stuff. Byron had 'is gun in the wagon. We put all our money together to make the 3 dollars. We bet that our Miss Sanders would win. We telled 'er we'd give 'er our share if'n she won.

People started comin' in. Miss Sanders had 'er pistol in the wagon. We put Charley in the barn and gived 'im some corn. He shore liked it.

'Bout 10 of the people was linin' up to shoot. They was people with fancy guns and clothes. And then they was Byron and me with no shoes on, but they didn't seem to care. We looked up and there stood the man that took us to Ocala.

He sed, "What's up, boys?"

We telled 'im, "Miss Sanders is a good shot with a pistol and she don't have no money, but we got 3 dollars and we want to bet on 'er. And if'n she wins we'll give it all to 'er"

He sed, "Is she that good?"

We sed, "We thank she is."

They shot shotguns, then they shot rifles, and then pistols come up. We telled Miss Sanders it were time for 'er to shoot. She sed she didn't have no money, but we telled 'er we done registered 'er.

They shot 20 yards and the one that hit the target best were the winner. They was bettin' on all the good shooters. When 'er turn come up to shoot, the man from Ocala sed he bet 100 dollars on Miss Sanders. Some of the shooters wanted to up it to 200 dollars. The man from Ocala agreed.

He sed, "Y'all boys keep your 3 dollars."

They was 5 shooters and ever'one of them fellers was real good. They was a man with a funny watch. It didn't keep time but it telled how fast they shot. I went down the line and ever'one had shot 'cept Miss Sanders.

She leveled 'er pistol up and the man sed, "Go bam-bam-bam-bam-bam."

I ain't never seen nobody shoot that fast. We didn't know if'n she won or not. I shore hope she had. They wrote the names on what they shot. The judge sed Miss Sanders had the fastest time. I shore hope she hit the target. Then they started measurin' every shot. I looked at Miss Sanders and she looked real happy.

The judged sed, "We got a winner!"

He jist looked 'round. I thought, why don't he jist tell us Miss Sanders is the best shot!

The man walked over to Miss Sanders and gived 'er the trophy. It shore looked nice! The man from Ocala gived 'er a bag with some money in it. I don't know how much, but some money is better than none.

Ever'body started to leave and the man from Ocala asked me what we was doin' next. He sed, "If'n y'all find someone new, let me know."

Then he handed me a bag and told me to split it with Byron.

We put the mower in the wagon and hitched up Charley. Mr. Keith come out and thanked us. Sed, "Y'all boys shook up a lot of people today. It were fun!"

Then he telled us he bet on Miss Sanders too. He gived us a bag to give to Miss Sanders with somethang in it. When we got to the dirt road she opened the bag from the Ocala man. They was 400 dollars in it.

Miss Sanders sed, "I can't take that much money!"

But we telled 'er that he wanted 'er to have it and to jist keep it. Then she opened the bag from Mr. Keith and they were 50 dollars in it. She cried. She tried to give it to us but we wouldn't take it.

It had been a long day, but a good day. We let 'er out at 'er house and out walked that sorry ole boy of 'ers. We taked Charley home and fed 'im and rubbed 'im down.

Later in life I thank of all the people we met along the way and the thangs they done for us. We had a charmed life!

In real life: Miss Sanders is a real person from my church.. She is a very nice lady and sits on the back row with 'er son. He's a real nice man and we call 'im "the candy man." He carries candy for the kids.

Red Fussell

Sugar Cane Field   Sandy Kruse

The MULE

Chapter 22

It were late in October and had done turned cold already. I were out by the hog pen. I built a fire to keep the hogs warm, when my dad walked up and sed, "Let's go to Lady Lake to look at a mule."

I told 'im I didn't want a big one. So we went to Lady Lake where the mule skinner lived. He had a bunch of mules. I told 'im I wanted a little mule.

He showed us some mules—some big and some little. I seen one over in the corner standin' all by 'imself. He were jist the right size. I asked the mule skinner 'bout 'im. Then he told us nobody can break 'im. He bites and kicks. Sed, "Y'all can't catch 'im. Some where down the line somebody beat 'im and he never forgot. I sold 'im 3 times and they all bring 'im back. But if'n y'all want 'im I'll jist charge you 25 dollars and I'll bring 'im to Okahumpka, but y'all can't bring 'im back."

So I asked my dad, "Do y'all thank we can break 'im?"

He looked at me and sed, "It's up to y'all to break 'im. It'll take time and y'all may never break 'im. But y'all can't never hit 'im."

The man sed, "20 dollars."

So I told 'im to take 'im and put 'im in the hog pen with the hogs that afternoon.

He bringed 'im to Okahumpa in the afternoon. That mule were mad! They backed up to the gate and unloaded 'im. He tried to bite and kick. But the man stayed clear.

I were gonna go git the money to pay for the mule but my dad had the money for 'im. He gived me a box of sugar in little sugar blocks and told me, "If'n this don't work, nothin' will."

When my dad went to pay for the mule, the skinner sed that if'n we do break 'im, he wanted to know how we done it. Then he telled my dad to jist pay 'im later.

I tried to give the mule sugar but he jist looked at me. My dad made a trough for feed and water. Then he telled me, "Don't hit 'im. Don't have a stick 'round 'im or a rake or a shovel. He's got to learn y'all won't hurt 'im."

The first week didn't look good, but I put a lump of sugar in 'is feed trough. He et it. The next day I put 'nother one there and he et it. Then he started lookin' for the lump of sugar. I had a bucket with a lump of sugar in it and a week later when he seen the bucket, here he come. Then I'd hold the bucket and he'd eat the sugar. Once he tried to bite me so I didn't give 'im no sugar. The next day he et the sugar and didn't try to bite me.

It kept gettin' better. When I'd walk out to the hog pen, here he come. I gived 'im a lump of sugar and touched 'im on the neck. He looked like he were gonna bite me and then he stopped, and I gived 'im the sugar. Ever' day it were somethin' new.

I'd had 'im for 'bout a month and I could touch 'im and rub 'is neck. If'n he tried to bite me then, no sugar. I tried to rub 'im on 'is back but he tried to bite me, so no sugar. He'd follow me all 'round the pen. He knowed what he done.

Byron come over and brought Charley up to the fence. Them two looked like ole lost friends. When Byron and Charley left my mule brayed, which he'd never done afore, and I could pet 'im now.

I went to Miss Sanders to see if'n I could buy the stuff in 'er barn, but she jist give it all to me. So I got Byron and Charley and we got the wagon and put all the farm stuff in it – the collar trace chain, all the plows and rake. Then we come back and got the buggy. It shore were nice.

Skeeters and Hogs and Mules, Oh My!

Now the hard part. I got the lump of sugar and gived it to my mule. I put a halter on 'im and he wanted 'nother lump of sugar and I gived it to 'im. I left the halter on for 2 days. I rubbed 'im on the neck. Afore, he used to try to bite me, but not now. Then I put the halter on 'im and put a rope on 'im and led 'im 'round the pen. Then I gived 'im a lump of sugar. I rubbed 'im on 'is back and he liked that. The next thang I done were to put the collar on 'im and gived 'im a lump of sugar.

My mama told me, "Y'all are gonna rot 'is teeth!"

But I were happy with what I were doin'. I hope nobody hit 'im. I got to where I could rub 'im down too.

The man from Lady Lake come by and I showed 'im what I could do with 'im, jist usin' a lump of sugar.

Then I put the trace chain on. He didn't like it, but he liked the sugar. After a while he were alright and I put the saddle blanket on. Then I put ever'thang on 'im and led 'im 'round the hog pen. He done real good.

I bringed out the shotgun and shot it out there. To start with he didn't like it, but I gived 'im a lump of sugar and he were alright. He'd come a real long way. I talked to 'im. I knowed he didn't know what I sed. I hadn't named 'im yet, but I shore were happy with 'im.

Then I got the idea that I'd ride 'im. So I put the halter on 'im and gived 'im a lump of sugar. I got 'im by the fence and crawled on 'is back. He didn't like it at all. He throwed me off in the hog waller. I were muddy all over. I looked up and guess who were lookin' at me—that mule, as if to say, "What are y'all doin' in the mud?"

At first I were mad. Then I laffed. I thought, *You crazy ole mule. You done it to me again!*

So I gived 'im a lump of sugar and he follered me to the mule lot. I taked the bridle off, fed 'im and rubbed 'im down. Then I laffed. I don't know why them mules is so dumb.

Then I taked a bath. I smelled real bad.

I got to where I would take my mule for a walk over to Byron's house. They's a pond behind Byron's house. I led the mule out to the pond. He seemed to like it. I told Byron to hold the rope and help me git on 'is back. So Byron took the rope and grabbed my foot and I climbed on 'is back. At first he just stood there. Then he tried to buck me off, but he couldn't buck in the water. Then Byron led 'im 'round the pond with me on 'is back. At first he didn't like it. Then he didn't seem to mind.

Byron then led 'im out of the pond and I got ready to git bucked off, but nothin' happened. I got off and rubbed 'im on the neck and gived 'im a lump of sugar. He were jist fine.

I picked up the halter up, crawled on 'is back and started home. He started to buck, but then he jist walked home. He stopped at the gate and I opened it. I taked off the halter and gived 'im a lump of sugar. Then he jist rolled in the dirt. I'd seen mules do that afore.

I tried to thank of a name and then all of a sudden, it come to me - Sugar.

Each day were somethin' new. Jist thank, if'n I hadn'ta got 'im, they woulda kilt 'im and made soap with 'im. He still had a long way to go, and I had yet to break 'im to plow. I ain't real shore 'bout that.

I tried it. I put the collar on Sugar and he jist looked at me. Then I hooked 'im up to the plow. My dad were watchin' to see what he'd do. Sugar jist looked at me so I gived 'im a lump of sugar.

He still jist looked at me. I told him, "Git up."

Then I tapped 'im with the rein and he eased up and we plowed a spot. I taked 'im back to the barn and put all the stuff in the barn and wiped 'im down. Then I gived 'im some sweet feed.

He could now pull the wagon and do what I wanted 'im to do. I shore liked that ole mule. Sometimes I would jist walk outside and he'd bray, kinda like he were glad to see me. I liked that.

Summer were goin' on. My dad come inside one mornin' and I seen the look on 'is face. I knowed somethang were wrong. He told me, "Y'all's mule died last night."

I run out to the barn and there he laid. So we dug a big hole and put 'im in it. Then the man down the road stopped by, and he helped me cover up the hole.

I walked over to Byron's and told 'im my mule died. I cried. Seems like everythin' I love dies. Uncle Will died. And now my mule died.

Skeeters and Hogs and Mules, Oh My!

Sugar the Mule   *Sandy Kruse*

The Night in the Swamp

Chapter 23

I asked Byron if'n he'd like to spend Friday night in the swamp in the tree house that we built.

He sed, "Shore."

So Friday when school let out I walked to the A&P Store and picked up some bad apples and peaches and anythang else we needed.

Byron stayed late at school, but I don't know why. So I caught a ride home and told my mama I were goin' to the swamp and that if'n I kilt a hog, I'd bring it home.

I walked over to Byron's house. If'n my mule hadn't a-died I'd a-rode 'im. Byron were waitin'. I had my .22 mag and he got 'is. We put most ever'thang in a feed sack and crossed the pond and walked on Stage Coach Road. Then we walked through the orange grove and looked back down the road. Here come Betty Jean, Byron's sister. Byron asked me if'n I cared if she went along.

I didn't care, but we told 'er that when we got to the tree house we had to stay. We had a flashlight, but didn't turn it on. We might need it later.

We set the hog trap. Hmm. Somebody had been usin' it. We could smell a dead hog. We kept some peaches that was good and we crossed the log. Byron sed he'd go up and see if'n they was any snakes or bugs in our tree house.

It were clear. So we built a fire so we could cook.

We bringed 2 sweet taters and 6 eggs. We got our fryin' pan and mashed the sweet taters and fried them in the fry pan. I made 3 plates out of a palmetto fan and put the sweet taters and fried eggs on it. We jist had one fork. It were the one we got from Uncle Will's house when he died. We jist passed it 'round. Mmm. That fry-up shore were good. We tried not to eat in the bed 'cause the ants would follow crumbs and find us.

Palmetto Leaf   *Sandy Kruse*

We got some stingin' nettles and boiled them and put some sugar on them. That way we made tea. We could strain it through the flour sack. We jist had one cup we got from Uncle Will's house too. We cut up some peaches and put them in the drink. We let Betty Jean try it first. She liked it. So we all drinked it.

It started to git dark so we put the fire out. It were a full moon, so we should have plenty of light. We had our sack bed up there but it had gotten flat. Thank we'll have to make a new one sometime.

It's always fun at night. They's all kind of noises jist at dark. The pine tree next to the tree house had died when lightnin' struck it a long time ago.

I asked Byron, "Do y'all thank they's another snake in this swamp?"

He sed, "I hope so, but I don't thank we should kill it."

It were jist 'bout dark and out walked a coon. I guess he went over to the hog trap and got 'im a peach.

They was noise ever'where. They was splashin' in the ditch, too. We couldn't see what it were, but we felt safe up high. That big ole cat come by, but he couldn't git us.

Then it got quiet. I didn't like that. Then they were some noise, but not much. Then the rain come and we knowed we was gonna git wet. But we built the cover to our tree house real good, so it didn't rain right on us. It shore did make noises.

Then the wind died down and it rained a little while longer. The swamp got its noise back. I slept 'bout all night. Betty Jean, she couldn't sleep at all. She sed they were jist too much noise.

I waked up 'bout daylight and we et some peaches. Byron sed, "Look! That looks like Ole Joe, the gator."

He shore were big! We hadn't seen anythang all night. I guess it were too much storm goin' on.

So we climbed down and walked over to the hog trap. We'd caught somethang, but it got out. We jist don't have much luck with that hog trap.

We climbed back up in our tree house, but not much come by, so we thought we might as well go home.

We looked 'cross the sawgrass. It looked like somethang big went through it. We walked back to Byron and Betty Jean's house. They telled us that a bad storm come through there.

I walked home and seen my dad had planted an orange tree where Sugar were buried.

He shore were a good mule. I miss 'im.

I took my bath and jist set on the porch.

I Didn't Do It

Chapter 24

Saturday rolled 'round with nothin' to do. So I told my mama, "I thank I'll go to the swamp."

I went to Byron's, but he went somewhere. I started to leave and Betty Jean wanted to know where I were goin'.

I told 'er, "To the swamp."

She asked if'n she could go.

I sed, "Shore." It's always good to have somebody in the swamp with y'all.

We waded 'cross the pond, walked down Stage Coach Road, crossed the orange grove and walked in on the log. It shore were quiet. But sometimes that's a bad sign. The sky were clear, so we climbed up to the tree house.

We'd been there 'bout an hour and nothin' come by. So we climbed down and walked by the hog trap.

Betty Jean told me, "They's a coon in the fork of that tree."

I shot the coon and skinned the hide off 'im. I shot 'im in the head so it wouldn't ruin the hide. I cut the lower part of the legs off and nailed the hide on a post. As soon as it dried I could make me a hat. They were a red ant bed at the bottom of the post and them ants would clean that skin real good in no time.

James Carlton Fussell

I put the coon in a flour sack to take to my mama. She'll cook it.

We walked to the spring and waded out in it. My! It shore felt good. We walked through the grove and et some oranges. Then I seen a rattlesnake under an orange tree. I asked Betty Jean if'n she'd like to shoot it. She didn't want to shoot, so I shot it. It had 6 rattles and a button. We jist left 'im there to rot.

We walked back down Stage Coach Road, waded 'cross the pond and stopped at the hog pen. They was some kids swingin'.

Betty Jean sed she were goin' home. So I walked 'cross the field and headed home too. My mama and Lewis Jr. was settin' on the porch. Lewis asked me what I kilt. I jist told 'im it were a coon.

I seen the look he gived me, and then he told my mama not to cook that coon.

She asked 'im why our house cat went missin'. Lewis sed he bet I shot it. So Mama asked me if'n I done somethin' to it.

I told 'er, "No." But I don't thank she believed me.

Then she told me she thought I fed it to the hogs. But I told 'er, "I shot a coon!"

She sed, "I'm not gonna take no chance and cook a house cat."

So I took the coon out back and fed it to the hogs. Two days later that ole tom cat come back home. By that time, I felt like shootin' 'im!

This is true. And I never skinned no house cat!

The "button" is the knob at the end of the rattles.
photo source: wallpapercave.com

Black Eyed Peas

Chapter 25

Miss Sweetie Pie stopped by and ask if'n Byron and me could pick the peas Saturday.

We told 'er, "Shore."

So Friday, on the school bus, we asked that red-headed girl that lives on Red Hill Grove if'n she wanted to pick too.

Byron picked 'er up Saturday 'bout 6 in the mornin'. Then he come by and picked me up. Ole Charley were shore slow. We went by Snell Dairy and went through woods. They had some people there to teach them how to can the peas.

They done washed a bunch of jars and we headed to the pea patch, but Miss Sweetie Pie told us to wash our feet and our hands and our face. The red-headed girl jist laffed. But Miss Sweetie Pie told us to go inside first.

We went inside and had a big breakfast. Mr. Mike set with 'is fork and knife. He were ready to eat. Over the years, Mr. Mike done et a bunch of them big breakfasts. He shore did like to eat, but he didn't like to work. I jist bet 'is mama left 'im a lot of money.

I here-tell that if'n Miss Sweetie Pie told 'im somethang he needed to do, and he didn't want to do it, that she hit 'im up the side of his head with the broom or a stick! I'd like to see that.

I et real quick and then we hit the pea patch. After a while we had a washtub full. We spread them peas on some paper on the porch to git them out of the sun and keep them from sweatin'. Miss Sweetie Pie told Mr. Mike to git 'im a pan and start shellin' them peas.

He looked at 'er real funny and then told 'er them peas hurt 'is fingers. She asked 'im which he wanted to hurt, 'is fingers or 'is head, and she picked up the broom.

Well, he got 'im a pan and started shellin' peas. That red-headed girl got 'er a pan. She shore knowed how to shell peas. But I woulda liked to see Miss Sweetie Pie hit 'im up the side of 'is head! I bet he woulda hollered loud.

Then Byron and me cut the okra and tamatas and the squash. We picked 'bout eve'thang in the garden. We picked the corn and then shucked the corn and fed the shucks to Charley. We left some ears in the shucks for 'im too.

They cut the corn off the cob and blanched it afore puttin' it in jars. Then they put a rubber ring on the top of the jars afore puttin' them in the pressure cooker.

It were gittin' late so we told Miss Sweetie Pie that our friend had to go home. Miss Sweetie Pie told Mr. Mike to take the red-headed girl home. She done worked hard all day. When she went to leave, Miss Sweetie Pie gived 'er a bunch of peas, corn, tators, squash, and tamatas, and we seen Mr. Mike give 'er some money too.

He taked 'er to Red Hill Grove. Then Miss Sweetie Pie wanted to know what she owed us. We told 'er that she had already paid us 'nough.

She gived Byron and me 2 big bags of stuff. My mama shore would be happy with that.

Then she telled us that Mr. Mike really is a good man and he worked hard, too, when he were young. And then she telled us that she really wouldn't hit 'im.

Miss Sweetie Pie telled us that when we git time, she'd like to have the garden plowed under. But we telled 'er that the okra would keep bearin' as long as it were kept cut, and that she could pick peas one more time. We still had the taters to do the next week.

It were gittin' dark, but we wasn't scared of no booger. I got home and gived the stuff to my mama. She shore were glad to git it.

But my brother telled me I could eat all that stuff. He liked fish best.

I taked a bath and went to bed.

Monday, when we was on the school bus, that red-headed girl telled us that Mr. Mike gived 'er 5 dollars and thanked 'er for helpin' 'im.

Scared

Chapter 26

We talked it over and sed we'd spend a night in the swamp on Friday. We'd fish in Shaw Pond and catch a good mess of bass. I don't know why they always say a "mess" of bass. They don't say they kilt a "mess" of quail or a "mess" of deer. But I guess that's alright.

We told Betty Jean she could help us cook them fish. And we invited the red-headed girl, but she sed her dad wouldn't let 'er. We asked RH and he sed he'd come. We'd bring some grits and some meal to make cornbread. We told RH to bring some tin plates. Byron's little brother wanted to come and I told Byron I didn't care.

So after school on Friday we left for the swamp with all that stuff in a flour sack. Saturday mornin' we fished all mornin' and got us that good mess of bass. Then we built a fire and got our cast iron fryin' pan out, and we got some swamp water. The fryin' pan were brown in the center but I cleaned it. We set the pot on the fire like I seen my mama do it and boiled the water to kill all the worms in the water.

Then we heerd someone holler and we hollered back. It were Paul from school. He were in the woods. Somebody told 'im we was cookin' in the woods.

We put the lard in the fryin' pan. It melted real quick and then it caught fire. We put a piece of tin on it to put the fire out. Then we raked ashed out to put the fryin' pan on. We put salt and pepper on the fish and dropped the fish in the hot lard. It cooked up real quick.

We had a big bunch of fish and I put them on our palmetto fan plates. Then we put the whole bag of grits in the pot and taked it off the fire. It poured out the top of the pot. I thank I put too much in it 'gain.

We mixed some of the grease in the cornmeal and put an egg in it. That one egg were all that ole hen laid. We put it in the fryin' pan and put a piece of tin on top. Then we put some ashes on top. It'll make it brown on top.

In a little while, we looked at the cornbread. Mmmm! It looked good. It were done already, so we cut it and got ready to eat.

Then it happened! The hair on my head stood straight up! That big ole cat screamed! It shaked the woods.

Byron and me grabbed our guns, but we couldn't see nothin'. We looked in the woods a bit, but we still couldn't see nothin'.

I told ever'body, "Let's git up in the tree house!"

I told Byron to watch while I got the food up to the tree house. We all got in the tree house. All 6 of us, Betty Jean, Larry, Paul, RH, Byron and me. We et the fish and the corn bread up there. I shore were full! It warn't as good as my mama made, but we et it. Puttin' some grease in the grits helped. It warn't bad.

Well, ever'thang were now quiet. Then the ole cat screamed again! It sounded like it were right on us. We can shoot it afore it gits us, but we don't see it.

We stayed in the tree house 'til it were gettin' late. Then we climbed down and walked out on the log. We looked in the grove but didn't see nothin'. We started out the grove on to Stage Coach Road and that cat jumped right 'cross the road.

Byron thought to shoot it, but it were gone, and it were big. He knowed where we was, but we didn't know where he were.

We crossed the pond and went home. I shore were glad to git back to the hog pen.

Byron told them all, "Don't tell nobody 'bout that cat. If our mamas find out, we won't git to go to the swamp!

James Carlton Fussell

All the times we went to the swamp after that we never seen the cat. Some people sed he comes through ever' year for a little bit.

Once while huntin' in the Green Swamp I seen a panther. That's a beautiful cat!

Red Fussell

Another Rainy Day

Chapter 27

The week passed fast and the weekend were comin' up. Me and Byron thought we should check on Miss Sander's cane patch.

So Saturday mornin' we hitched up Charley and taked the tools out to 'er cane patch. It looked like rain, but Charley didn't care.

We got to Miss Sander's house, put Charley in her barn and gived 'im some hay and wiped 'im down. He always liked that. I still thank he'd look good dyed green.

The clouds was buildin' up in the west. Then the wind started blowin'. I thought, *I don't think we can do much with the cane patch today.*

So I sed, "Byron, maybe we should go home."

We hitched Charley back up, picked up our tools and telled Miss Sanders we should go home. She tried to git us to stay, but we left. We had 'bout 2 miles to go to git to Byron's house and the rain already started. I don't thank Charley liked it, but he didn't git in no hurry. The driest thang we had was our tongues!

We finally got to Byron's house. The wind had got high and the trees was goin' ever' which way. I telled Byron I needed to git home.

It were hard walkin' in the rain and wind. When I got home the big oak in our yard had blowed down and my mama had pots and buckets to catch water ever'where the roof leaked. The boat were floatin' in the front yard and the dog were under the house to keep out of the rain. I don't know how much it rained, but it come down all day!

I changed my clothes. We jist et cold fish. I went to bed. Lewis, Jr. didn't go nowhere. The weather were jist too bad. The thunder and lightnin' were ever'where. The trees was a-twistin' and a-turnin'. My dad told me it were a bad storm and he were glad I come home.

It blew and rained all night. They was a bunch of water on the ground. I ain't seen so much rain!

The next day it stopped rainin' but they closed the school. The busses couldn't run. So I walked over to Byron's. The road were real muddy. I asked Byron if'n he wanted to go to the swamp to see if'n our tree house were still there.

So we taked our .22 rifles with us. They was lots more water in the pond in back of Byron's house. It were 'bout waist deep. We knowed we'd git wet. Stage Coach Road had water on it. Byron told me to stop and he shot a big ole snake. I guess it floated right where he were.

When we got to the orange grove, the wind had blowed most of the oranges off the trees. They was all over the ground. We walked through the grove and walked to the log where we walk in, and then we stopped. They was snakes ever'where.

I telled Byron, "I don't wanna go in there."

He sed he would. I heard 'im shoot 4 or 5 times and then he come back out. He sed, "They's snakes ever'where, but I didn't see no rattlesnakes, and our tree house looks good. It'll need some work, and 'bout ever'thang inside were wet."

They was snakes on the edge of the grove and we shot all we seen. Then we walked to Cason Hammock. A bunch of trees blowed down there. We seen a black snake. Then we heard a buzz tail rattlesnake and Byron shot 'is head off.

We walked through the grove, down Stage Coach Road, then to the clay road. They was a man walkin' down the clay road. He asked if'n we knowed anybody that could pull 'im out of a mud hole.

Byron telled 'im he had a mule that could pull 'im out. So we went to Byron's house and left our guns there. We walked down past the curve and seen the car in the mud.

Skeeters and Hogs and Mules, Oh My!

We hitched the traces to the front bumper and Charley pulled 'im out with no problem. We unhooked the traces and moved from out in front of the car. He started the car and taked off. He didn't even say, "Thank y'all!"

I telled Byron, "He must be a Yankee! That's the way they do!"

We walked back to Byron's house and washed the clay off Charley and wiped 'im down and dried 'im off. I still thank he'd look good green.

Our legs was yellow from walkin' in the red clay. I were tired and telled Byron I were goin' home.

I taked a bath to git the clay off me. Then I telled my dad what the man done. He jist sed that some people is jist like that, and they probably never done nothin' to help nobody else. He sed, "Don't worry 'bout it."

We seen that man again one day and he jist turned 'is head the other way and walked away. Byron pointed 'is finger at 'im and sed, "Bam!"

I jist laffed.

This last part didn't really happen.
Red Fussell

Muddy Road

Chapter 28

The school were still closed. The bus couldn't go down the clay roads with all that mud and water. So I walked over to Byron's house. It were still rainin' jist a little bit. We talked 'bout goin' over to the ditches to fish. When storms come, the fish go to the ditches.

A man stopped at Byron's house and asked Byron's dad if'n he pulled people out of the mud. Byron's dad told 'im he had a mule and would send the boys.

We put the trace chain on Charley and walked by Miss Sander's house 'bout half a mile past the Red Hill Grove. They was a car in the ditch. It slide off the road. And guess who it were --- that man we pulled out afore that didn't even tell us, "Thank y'all."

He seen us and sed if'n we pulled 'im out he'd pay us. We jist walked on by 'im.

Jist down the road were a lady stuck in the mud. We hitched Charley to 'er car and pulled 'er out. She thanked us and then she told us she didn't have no money to pay us.

We told 'er that it were alright.

She drove off and went right by the man in the ditch.

They was a pick-up truck in the ditch, so we pulled 'im out. He

Skeeters and Hogs and Mules, Oh My!

asked us how much. We told 'im whatever he wanted to give would be fine. He asked what the lady paid.

We told 'im, "She didn't have no money, but we told 'er it were alright. But she thanked us, and that were good."

He gived us 3 dollars. That would buy Charley some feed.

We now had ever'body out 'cept the same man in the ditch. We went back to where he were stuck and we stopped.

He telled us he'd give us one dollar if'n we'd pull 'im out.

We telled 'im, "Bye."

We started to leave and we was laffin'. Here he were standin' out in the mud and 'is car were still stuck.

Then he telled us, "Y'all is crooks."

So I telled 'im, "10 dollars."

He sed he wouldn't pay that.

I telled Byron, "Let's go home."

Then he sed, "2 dollars."

We sed, "Nope."

I sed, "Let's go, Byron."

Then the man telled us he didn't have much money.

We telled 'im. "If'n y'all had sed, 'Thank y'all' the last time, we woulda did it for nothin', but since y'all didn't, y'all have to pay."

He looked at the money he had in 'is pocket. It were jist 4 dollars. He sed it were all he had.

So we hitched Charley and pulled 'im out. We was 'bout as muddy as we could git. We got 'im to the center of the road and we got Charley unhitched.

The man spun 'is tires and throwed mud all over us. Byron held Charley 'cause he tried to run.

The man in the car shook 'is fist at us and 'is car slid sideways and back in the ditch. He were stuck again!

I got me a handful of clay. When we walked by 'im I hit 'im in the side of the head. Talk 'bout a mad man!!!

He sed he were gonna beat the devil out of us.

We walked on. We jist got to Byron's house when that man drove by. Somebody must a pulled 'im out. We thought he were gonna stop, but he didn't.

We taked Charley to the pond and washed 'im. Then we got most of the mud off us.

I telled Byron, "I thank that man got mad!"

The clay road were bad when it rained, and when it were dry it were dusty. Years later they paved it. It is now Hwy 470. Someday it will be 4 lanes.

They always say, "If'n you walk in the clay road when it's wet, it'll spread your toes."
Red Fussell

The Mud Hole

Chapter 29

The week passed fast and school were 'bout out. I'll be glad! I talked it over with Byron and we thought we'd git the weeds out of Miss Sander's cane patch since we couldn't do it the last Saturday.

So on Saturday we hitched up Charley. We decided we'd pick up the red-head girl if'n 'er daddy'd let 'er go.

We rode out to Red Hill Grove. That road were still muddy. Right out in front of 'er house they was a bad ole mud hole. I asked Byron if'n he wanted to go swimmin' in it.

He jist sed, "Not today."

When we got to 'er house, guess who were there – 'er boyfriend, Clem.

I told Byron, some day we're gonna have to fight 'im.

Clem told us, "Git."

I whispered to Byron, "Let's throw 'im in the mud hole."

And Byron sed, "Okay. Let's do it."

We kept eggin' 'im on and got 'im close to the mud hole. Then we both run at 'im and it throwed 'im off balance. He were headed to the hole, but he were holdin' on to me and I went in the mud hole with 'im.

We was some sight to see. Byron were laffin'. I told Clem, "Let's throw 'im in the mud hole."

So we run 'im down, grabbed Byron and put 'im in the mud hole. Then we seen a man comin' in a car.

He stopped as sed, "What y'all boys doin'?"

We telled 'im we was swimmin' in the mud hole.

I telled Byron, "If'n he gits out of 'is car, we'll put 'im in the mud hole." But he drove off.

We looked up and that red-headed girl's brother wanted to know what we was doin'. We telled 'im to come and see what we found.

When he got close 'nough we put 'im in the mud hole.

He sed 'is mama would kill 'im for gettin' 'is clothes wet. Well, not only was they wet, they was full of clay!

Here come 'nother car. It were RH with 'is mama. RH went to school with us back in grade school at Okahumpka. He got out to see what we was doin'. We grabbed 'im and threw 'im the mud hole.

I already knowed my mama were gonna make me wash my own clothes. We was muddy from head to toe and RH's mama sed he could jist walk home!

They was lots of noise here now, and here come that red-headed girl.

Byron sed, "Let's throw 'er in the mud hole, Clem."

She wanted to know what we was doin'. Byron telled 'er we was swimmin'.

We looked down the road and here come Miss Sander's son. He were next. He were close to the hole and Byron gived 'im a shove. He grabbed that red-headed girl and she were in the mud hole too. She even sed a bad word.

It wouldn't a-been so bad, but ever'body laffed. She didn't thank it were funny!

We was all 'bout as muddy as we could be. We seen 'nother car comin' and we all got in the mud hole with jist our heads stickin' up. They stopped the car and the woman wanted to know what we was doin'. We telled 'er we was jist swimmin'.

She stepped out of the car, slipped in the mud and fell down. Now she were muddy too. She got up and got back in 'er car. She were sayin' lots of bad words.

We looked up and we seen a truck comin'. The fender were a rattlin'.

Skeeters and Hogs and Mules, Oh My!

I told Byron, "That's Jack and Judy from Clear Water Lake."

We all got in the mud hole and left jist our head stickin' out. When Judy seen us she told Jack to stop.

He told 'er, "No."

The she told 'im, "Stop this truck!"

So he stopped. Then he told Judy, "We can't stay. We stole 'em chickens on the back of the truck. We shore don't wanna git caught."

She walked over to see what we was doin'. When she got next to the mud hole she slipped in the hole. She went under the water. When she come up ever'body were laffin', but now she sed some bad words.

Then Jack told 'er to git in the back of the truck. He warn't gonna let 'er git that mud in 'is truck. We watched them ride off.

We played in the mud some more and then I seen 4 boys comin'. We knowed Larry and Bill. They had 2 other brothers with 'em. Well, we was all in the hole 'gain with jist our heads stickin' out when they walked up.

They wanted to know what we was doin'. Byron and Clem got out. We told them to look in the hole, so they walked to the edge. It were too late. Byron and Clem pushed them in the hole and they was muddy too.

Larry sed, "I knowed we shouldn't a stopped!" He jist knowed 'is mama were gonna tan they's hide for gettin' they's clothes muddy.

They climbed out and was really muddy. We all jist laffed.

They left to go home. That'll teach them to stop.

I wish somebody'd come by and take our picture. It were hard to keep our clothes on with all that clay stickin' to us. It made our clothes heavy.

The red-headed girl went in the house. We told ever'body that they's a big spring 'cross the road. So we crossed the road and over the fence to the spring. It shore had clear water and we shucked our clothes off and got in. The spring done turned yellow with all the clay we washed off. We washed and beat our clothes on a log to git the clay off of 'em. We did git most of it out.

If'n we'd had some matches we coulda built a fire and dry our clothes, but had to put 'em back on wet.

We went back through the fence to the road. Guess who were standin' there. That red-headed girl's dad. I jist knowed we'd had it then!

He started to say somethang, and then he jist laffed. He turned and walked away!

The red-headed girl come out where we had Charley tied to an orange tree. She asked what her dad sed. We telled 'er he thought it were funny.

Clem sed, "That's the most fun I've had in a long time."

We asked 'im if'n he wanted to help us weed Miss Sander's cane patch. With all of us workin' together, we'd git it done real quick.

We all got on the wagon and rode to Mr. Hall's store. Clem bought us all a cold drink and he got one for that red-headed girl. Then we rode back to Red Hill Grove.

Clem married that red-headed girl.
Red Fussell

A Mud Hole   *Sandy Kruse*

Rooster

Chapter 30

They's a new family moved in on the clay road jist this side of the first curve. We heerd 'is name were Ed, and he were gone a lot. His wife's name were Peg, but I don't know what they's last name is.

We knowed she put a posted sign on ever' tree. They put up a fence to keep they's dog in. They done got it from the pound. I don't know what a pound is, but they say it's free.

A week after she got the dog she let 'im in the house and he chewed up 'er couch. So he went back to the pound. I guess they wanted 'im back.

Then we heerd she got somethang else to guard 'er yard when she were gone.

They's a man in Okahumpka that steals whatever he can and she knowed 'bout 'im.

So she got chickens. Well, that won't stop nobody!

One night she heerd a loud noise in the chicken house. She got 'er gun and headlight and put a buck shot shell in 'er gun. She went to the chicken house and guess what she seen. There set Ralph with the chickens. He were settin' real still. Mrs. Peg had a stick in 'er hand.

They was the rooster in there with Ralph, and if'n he moved that ole

James Carlton Fussell

rooster went after 'im.

Ralph told Mrs. Peg to call off the rooster, but she told 'im, "See y'all in the mornin'."

And she went back to bed.

When she woke up she were laffin'. She knowed he had a bad night.

She stopped Mr. Antz, the mailman to show 'im. And Mr. Antz laffed too, and he telled ev-er'body what he seen.

Then Peg taked the buck shot out of the gun and put bird shot in 'er gun. She got 'er stick and run the rooster in a different pen and locked the door.

Then she telled Ralph to git out. He'd had a long night.

Ralph sassed 'er, but she telled 'im to run if'n 'she didn't jist shoot 'im.

He telled 'er she wouldn't shoot 'im, but she raised the gun and shot between 'is feet. Then she raised the gun and looked 'im stright in 'is eyes. He turned and run.

When he got 'bout 30 yards away she shot. He hollered and knowed he'd been hit. She telled 'im, "Don't come back!"

Ever'time someone asked Ralph 'bout the chicken house, he telled them, "Ain't none of y'all's business."

We got to where we stopped by jist to make shore that rooster were in the pen.

Her husband come home late one night and the rooster put 'im up a ladder. He were jist a-hollerin' for Peg.

So if'n y'all see a sign that says, "Watch out for the rooster", y'all better thank twice afore y'all enter.

This is a different Peg from the one in the other books.
Red Fussell

Skeeters and Hogs and Mules, Oh My!

Mr. Hormer

Chapter 31

Mr. Hormer stopped by Byron's house and asked 'im if'n he'd like to pick 'is corn. He had a big ole patch. He raised it for 'is hogs and chickens. He had a corn crib like Byron's Uncle Kocker.

Byron asked 'im what he paid. Mr. Hormer told 'im he could have a wagonload of corn.

Byron come to ask me if'n I'd do it. He told me that Charley would eat the corn. So we agreed to pick.

Mr. Hormer were goin' to Tampa for 'bout a week, but he shore would like to have 'is corn picked afore it rained.

So we asked 'im which row we could pick for us to keep. He told us, "The short row."

Well, the coons done et most of that one.

He left on Monday. After school we looked at the corn patch. I telled Byron, "Let's fill our wagonload first."

Byron agreed. We pulled and shucked till dark. Then we put it in the crib. The next night we done the same. The crib were full so we put some in a barrell. We picked ever' day after school.

Mr. Hormer's crib were 'bout full too, and they were one row left to pick when he come home.

We telled 'im we was gonna pick our corn 'cause 'is crib was full.

He sed, "Jist put y'all's in a sack. That last row is y'all's."

They was hardly any corn on it. I telled Byron, "I'm shore glad we got ours first." We telled 'im we wasn't gonna pick no more. They wasn't no corn on that outside row.

Mr. Hormer sed, "Take it, or leave it."

We had some corn in the wagon and jist telled 'im, "Bye."

But he telled us to unload what corn we had in the wagon.

I telled Byron, "Let's go." And we drove the mule out the gate.

He telled us, "I shore won't hire y'all to work for me no more!"

We taked the shelled corn and put it in a sack and beat it with a hammer 'til we had the corn all breaked up. We had 'bout a sack full. I gived it to my mama to feed the chickens.

'Bout 2 or 3 days later we seen that same man comin' our way. He wanted us to come back and pick the rest of the corn. He sed we could have part of it. So we agreed.

We got 'im a load and then we pulled us a load. He telled us, "That's way too much corn for y'all to take!"

So I telled Byron, "Let's quit! It ain't worth it."

We started to leave and he sed, "Hey, where y'all goin with my corn?"

I telled Byron, "Don't even look back!"

He telled ever'body we stole 'is corn. But if'n he knowed we'd filled our crib, he'd really woulda been mad!!

Durin' this time lots of grownups and kids
worked and didn't git paid.
Red Fussell

The Cotton Patch

Chapter 32

Mrs. Hall had a cotton patch. She got 'bout all the kids in Oka-humpka to pick cotton for 'er and she paid us a penny a pound. It were hard to pick. She had a bunch of people pickin' at the same time. I made 'bout a dollar and 50 cents all day long. Some made more and some made less. But it were better'n nothin'.

RH found a black snake out there. His step dad caught snakes for a livin' so RH waren't 'fraid of no snake. He had it in 'is hand and walked towards a black lady. She told 'im she'd cut off 'is head if'n he put that snake on 'er.

She had a straight razor open. We all seen it. I ain't never seen no-body kilt, but Mrs. Hall put a stop to it. She told RH to go home, and we all went back to work.

It come a small rain and then the sun come out 'gain. It got real hot. The shade shore woulda felt good, but if'n y'all are in the shade y'all won't make no money.

The next day RH come back. Mrs. Hall told 'im if'n he picked up more snakes he'd have to leave and not come back.

I picked cotton all week and made 4 dollars. We picked the whole field and they's 'nother field north of Bridges Road.

When we stopped at lunch, Bobby and I stripped our clothes off and went swimmin' in the mule lot. Bobby's sister were 2 years older than us. She got 'her a switch and put it on our behinds and told us to put our clothes on. And we done it!

That afternoon it shore were hot. They was a black lady pickin' cotton too. She had dress on and then pants under 'er dress. She got a stingin' ant in them pants, and she shucked them pants right off! Them ants hurt.

The cotton pickin' day were over. They didn't grow cotton in Oka-humpka very long. Them old cotton boles was hard on y'all's hands.

Skeeters and Hogs and Mules, Oh My!

Jist 'Nother Week

Chapter 33

The week passed by real quick. I shore am glad my mama don't make me carry no s'rup bucket with my lunch in it to school. Sometimes I thank them rich kids had ever'thang, but then I'm glad I got what I got.

The ole house we lived in didn't even keep the rain off us. But it were the best we could do and y'all should be proud of what y'all have. We had plenty to eat. The winters was cold and the summers was hot.

When y'all never have nothin', y'all don't miss it.

My dad and Uncle Will taught me how to live by y'all's wits – how to skin a hog, how to kill food to eat, and if y'all can kill somethang jist for the fun of killin' it - don't do it.

Even in later year I lived by that rule.

I kilt my share of snakes and I love to frog hunt. Byron and me done skinned many gators and we skinned hogs and lived off the land.

I love the fun we had with Uncle Will. He lasted 'bout 84 years, best I can tell. He's been gone a long time now and we still miss 'im.

I wrote this 'cause I jist had 'im on my mind.
Thank y'all, Uncle Will for all y'all taught me.
Red Fussell

Guess How

Chapter 34

They's a new family moved in at Wigon Pond. They bought 'bout 3 acres and asked Byron if'n we'd mow it for them.

He told them that we'd mow it on Saturday. So Friday night we put the mower in the wagon. All we needed to do were to hook up Charley the next mornin'.

Byron told me he'd pick me up 'bout 6 in the mornin'. We et afore we left 'cause they didn't have no house there yet. They wanted to have it mowed so they could build a small house on the land.

We went by Snell Dairy. We coulda gone down 27, but it were easier to go through the woods, and Charley done better on the dirt road. It taked us 'bout 45 minutes to git there.

Ole Charley don't git in no hurry.

Byron brought Betty Jean to help rake the grass we mowed. We saved it all for Charley. Now we'd have a hay stack. We taked the mower out of the wagon and the man showed us where he wanted us to mow.

'Bout noon it were all mowed. We bringed us 2 sweet taters for lunch. We taked the peelin' off and divided it up. My mama gived me 2 sugar cookies and we split them up. Not a bad lunch. We had a jug of water and Byron led Charley to the pond so he could git a drink of

Skeeters and Hogs and Mules, Oh My!

water. Then Byron stopped in 'is tracks.

He sed. "Bring my gun. They's a big snake here."

He backed Charley back and shot the snake. It were a big ole cottonmouth. I were shore glad he were dead.

The people that owned the place was glad it died too. They telled us they's from Alabama and they didn't talk like us. He telled us 'is name were Steve and her name were Pam.

We raked up the grass. They even helped us and we telled them that Charley would eat it. Steve asked us how much money we wanted for mowin'. We jist telled 'im whatever he wanted to pay us were fine.

He gave Byron $3 and he gave me $3. We was happy with that.

On the way home I telled Byron, "Them people shore don't look like people that live in the woods."

The weekend rolled 'round and I telled Byron to go over to where they's buildin' the house. When we got there they had dried it in. It were a little house and the rooms was little. It were jist a shell and they had a wood stove. They drilled a shallow well and had a pitcher pump, and they built an outhouse. They put a bobwire fence all 'round the place.

I telled Byron, "They had to have help to do all this since last week."

They had a real nice car. It were all covered up. They asked Byron if'n he were good with the gun.

Byron sed, "I hit what I shoot at."

Then they asked if'n we knowed Henry and where did he live?

We telled 'im he lived on Dilly Lake, but he don't like nobody 'round 'is house, so we stayed 'way.

He looked at 'is wife and jist shook 'is head.

We left and went by Mr. Mike's house. He were sittin' on the porch. He sed, "Boys, come on up and have a seat."

He asked what we'd been doin', and we telled 'im we'd been over to Wigon Pond.

He looked real funny. He telled us, "Y'all best stay 'way from them."

We asked 'im why, and he sed, "They come here to kill somebody, but nobody knows who."

He sed, "They's bad."

We telled 'im, "They was real good to us."

He still telled us to stay 'way from 'em. He got us a drink and then wanted to know who the girl were with us.

We telled 'im, "Betty Jean, Byron's sister."

We thanked 'im, and he telled us to stay away from them people, but to come by 'is house any time.

The week passed with not much goin' on. We was at Mr. Hall's store and they was talkin'. They found a man dead on the side of the road. He'd been wanted in New York for shootin' a man. They even burnt 'is house down out on Dilly Lake. They didn't know who done it.

A big ole car showed up in Okahumpka and the man wanted to know who got shot and where he lived. It warn't Steve. This man had a driver with a funny lookin' hat.

I telled Byron, "We need to stay 'way from them people."

In 'bout 3 days my dad telled me they found a big ole car with 2 dead people in it. They'd been set on fire. Some sed they seen it at Mr. Hall's store.

I telled Byron, "Thank they could be Steve and Pam?"

He sed, "Shore do, but I don't wanna go and see."

Some sed, "They's the ones that done it."

When the law went to check on them, he sed they didn't do it. Sed they was G-men and they was lookin' for some people who robbed 3 banks in New York.

I shore were glad it warn't Steve and Pam done it. They seem like nice people.

I telled Byron, "Let's go see 'em."

We hooked up Charley and went through the woods. They was gone. The grass growed and caught fire and burned the house down.

I shore would like to know if'n did it kill them people?

The Blueberry Patch

Chapter 35

School were closed. Dale stopped and asked if'n Byron and me wanted to pick blueberries. He paid 15 cents a bucket. But he telled us we couldn't eat any while we was pickin'. Well, we never picked blueberries afore. But we knowed that if'n Dale turned 'is back, we'd eat some anyway.

He picked us up on Monday 'bout 7 in the mornin'. My mama fixed me a lunch and put it in a s'rup bucket like my dad's. She put a sweet tater for Byron in there too. He shore likes them sweet taters. We put our lunch in the shade to keep the sun off it.

They was some people there to pick some berries for themselves. They had 4 girls. One were a red-head. She were mad as fire. It's a wonder 'her hair didn't catch on fire she were so mad. They wouldn't let 'er pick blueberries. They sed she had to be 12 to pick and she wouldn't be 12 for another month. She were jist a-fumin'.

We asked Dale why they wouldn't let 'er pick, and he sed she might git hurt.

We picked blueberries 'til noon and made 'bout 4 dollars, which warn't too bad. But we had to keep them blueberries cool so they wouldn't start to mold.

We stopped for lunch. I gived Byron 'is sweet tater and he et it right up.

I asked Dale if'n I could pick some berries for my mama.

He sed, "Shore."

So I picked 'er a bag full. Then we got in 'is truck and he taked us back to Okahumpka.

That really happened. The red-headed girl were Sandy
And she is still mad 'bout not gittin' to pick.
Red Fussell

Dale and chickens   *Red Fussell*

The Cantalopes

Chapter 36

The milkman come by Byron's house and wanted to know if'n we'd haul 'is cantalopes to 'is house at the dairy. He told us he paid 1 cent per cantalope.

Byron asked me if'n we should, 'cause he don't like to pay, but I sed, "If'n he don't we can git even when we put soap in all 'is milk bottles."

We thought we'd haul one load, and if'n he don't pay us, we wouldn't haul no more.

Well, school were out, so on Monday we started at daylight. The milkman were cuttin' the cantalope off the vines already. We loaded the wagon and when it were full, we taked it to the dairy and put 'em under the oak tree.

We counted every load. We hauled 4 loads and was really tired. So we told 'im how many cantalopes we hauled and what he owed us.

He tried to tell us it were per load, not per cantalope. Well, they was a man standin' there and he told the milkman that warn't what he told us.

The milkman told 'im to keep 'is mouth shut.

We seen the look on that man's face and he balled up 'is fist and walked over to the milkman. He sed, "Pay the boys!"

The milkman were a big ole man, but the other man didn't care. He told 'im 'gain to pay us. The milkman grabbed 'is shirt. Well, he shouldn'ta did that! The man hit the milkman right in the nose and blood jist flied!

The milkman jumped up and the man knocked 'im down 'gain, and once more he sed, "Pay the boys!"

Well, he owed us 7 dollars.

The milkman picked up a stick, but he were too late and the man hit 'im 'gain and told 'im to pay us 7 dollars. He finally done it.

We told the milkman that we warn't gonna work for 'im no more! We walked to the wagon and thanked the man for takin' up for us. We both got 3 dollars and Charley got a dollar for feed.

MR. MIKE

Chapter 37

It were Wednesday. It looked like a dry day so we loaded up the wagon and tied the mower on the back. We thought we'd go over to Mr. Mike's and plow up 'is taters and pick the dry corn for Charley.

We got there, but nobody were home. We still taked the mower and mowed the corn stocks down and pulled the dry corn off the stock.

We plowed up the taters. They was a bunch of them, and they was a good size. We had 2 wash tubs full. So we got some moss and wiped the dirt off. We didn't wanna wash 'em with water 'cause they'd rot.

While I were cleanin' 'em, Byron pulled the tamata plants up. He telled us he got a lot of them. The okra hadn't been cut like it shoulda been, so it quit makin' more okra, and the peas done dried up. So we picked them.

We put them peas in a flour sack and beat 'em with a stick. Then we taked the bad parts out. They had a good mess. They'd have to pick out the wormy ones, or they could jist cook 'em and strain off the worms.

When we cook in the woods we jist eat 'em. We can't tell no difference.

We cleaned out most of the trash and then Byron plowed. Then he taked the drag to level out the ground. I raked down the bad spots.

When we was workin' we seen quails walkin' in the grass. I telled Byron, "We should bring our traps over here and catch 'em quail. We could put 'em in the wagon and nobody would see 'em."

But Byron sed, "We'd better ask Mr. Mike. He may be feedin' 'em to jist look at."

I telled Byron, "We eat 'em. Mr. Mike shoots all the rabbits. They eat 'is garden."

We had 'bout all the garden done, so we hooked up the mower and mowed all the field and 'round the house. It shore looked good. Then we put all the stuff from the garden on the porch.

I telled Byron that we should git us some taters, so we both got us a little bag.

It looked like rain, so we loaded up the wagon. If'n we put the hay up wet it would jist rot and be no good, so we jist left it on the ground.

The dark clouds was buildin'. When we left, them clouds got darker and darker and the lightnin' and thunder got started. It were loud, but it didn't bother Charley a bit. And then the rain come! We was as wet as 2 drowned rats.

Byron let me off at the house. I walked inside and my mama were puttin' pots where the house leaked. I taked off my wet clothes and put on some dry ones. They shore felt good. Shore am glad to git 'is garden done.

The next day Mr. Mike and Mrs. Sweetie Pie stopped by.

They wanted to know how much they owed us.

We telled them, "Nothin'."

They sed, "Well, it shore looks good!"

We telled them we got us some taters, and they sed that were jist fine.

Then I asked Mr. Mike if'n we could put our traps out to catch the quail.

He asked, "Is it against the law?"

I looked at Mr. Mike and sed, "We ain't never been caught."

Mr. Mike sed, "But if'n y'all put them traps out there and they found them, who would go to jail?"

We laffed and I sed, "Y'all."

Mrs. Sweetie Pie sed, "Put them traps out."

Skeeters and Hogs and Mules, Oh My!

Mr. Mike jist laffed.

> All them years that we trapped quail
> we never got caught once.
> Red Fussell

Florida quail

FISHIN' WITH A STICK

Chapter 38

We was settin' at Mr. Hall's store. I asked Byron if'n he wanted to go fishin'.

He sed, "Shore."

So we headed to Wallet Pond. We knowed the back side of the pond were 'bout dry, but we could git us a pine root to stir up the mud and them fish'll come to the top. We could jist hit the fish to kill 'em and put 'em in a flour sack. Some times we'd git a bunch, and sometimes nothin'.

We walked down the railroad track and climbed through the fence. They's a posted sign to stay out on jist 'bout ever' post, 'cause that man didn't like nobody to fish in 'is pond. But when 'is cows git out, he wants us to help 'im git 'em back in.

It were a good sunny afternoon. We picked up RH to go with us and got to the pond.

When y'all wade in that mud, y'all's legs itch when y'all come out, so then we'll go to the big pond to wash off the mud.

We started stirrin' the mud. We didn't see no fish, but a snake shore come to the top. We backed out of the pond. They was snakes ever'where.

Skeeters and Hogs and Mules, Oh My!

RH sed, "Them ain't bad snakes."

I didn't know how he knowed by jist lookin' at 'em, but I seen that he didn't stay in the mud neither.

We went to the big pond to wash the mud off. We looked up and here come some big boys. They was gonna seine fish that ole muddy pond, so we follered 'em to watch.

They had a big piece of chicken wire and put a post down in the mud, tied one end of the net to the post and put the other end on they's ole truck. We was watchin'. They didn't know that hole were full of snakes, and we shore didn't tell 'em.

They had a window weight on the bottom of the chicken wire. Then they started up the truck to pull the line up the bank to git the fish in the net. Well, we didn't want no part of them snakes.

Mud Puppies

They got their sacks ready. They pulled the net up on the bank, and then they all taked off runnin'. They'd done pulled up nothin' but snakes, and them snakes was goin' ever'where y'all could thank of.

They couldn't git the seine loose from the truck, so the driver jist stepped on the gas. It pulled the post out of the ground, pullin' the wire with all them snakes tryin' to git out.

RH telled us, "Them ain't snakes. They's mud-puppies or eels."

Well, they shore looked like snakes to me, but when they got on the ground, they couldn't crawl. They was tryin' to git back in the water.

But they was some nice bass left on the bank. RH picked them up. Me and Byron warn't gonna go where them mud-puppies was. They was ever'where.

The big boys done left and we had their fish. We had a good mess, so we cleaned all the bass and gived Mr. Hall a good mess.

I didn't take none home. If'n my dad knowed I caught 'em in a mud pond, he wouldn't want none anyway.

A few days later we went back and the buzzards was havin' a good meal.

They was a black man from the Quarters standin' there, and he sed, "Them mud-puppies is good to eat."

When I was in Hong Kong I tried eatin' mud-puppies.
I shore didn't thank they was at all good.
Red Fussell

COON HUNTIN'

Chapter 39

The watermelons was comin' in, and the coons moved in on the field to eat. It wouldn'-a been so bad, 'cept they jist eat a hole in a melon and then run to 'nother one.

So Mr. Shaw, who owned the field, called Jack. Jack had some dogs that was good for huntin' coon. He lived out on Taveres Highway.

Friday night Jack showed up with 'bout 10 dogs. It were afore dark. Mr. Shaw asked Byron and me if'n we'd like to go out there, too.

Instead of goin' barefooted like we always done, we put shoes on. They had snake-proof boots on. They'd never been snake bit and didn't want to, neither.

We loaded up at the store, so Byron and me rode out with Mr. Shaw. We went past Mule-Head Lake. It were 'bout dark when we got there.

Then they let the dogs out next to a small lake. The lead dog let out a bark and the rest got goin'. They had a race goin' on.

They headed towards Twin Lake. That coon were on a run! Then we heerd the dog bay.

The coon were up a pine tree.

We looked for the coon, then someone seen 'is eyes. One man handed Byron 'is rifle. Byron shot and the coon fell. The dog grabbed 'im and kilt 'im.

They throwed the dead coon on top of the dog box in the back of the truck. Then we all walked through the woods to find 'nother coon track.

"Bout that time the ole Blue Tick hound opened up with a loud bark and the race were on 'gain. Them dogs was shore good dogs. They taked us south of Mulehead Lake and by the mule lot. The coon were movin' fast. They's a small island on the north side.

Then we heerd them dogs bay when they'd treed the coon. We waded out to the island. Them dogs was lookin' in a big oak tree and somethin' was tryin' to hide in the moss.

Then Jack shined a light up there and sed, "Don't shoot. That's a bob cat."

They caught the dogs and put 'em on leashs. They wouldn't shot a bob cat. He gits the rats and rabbits.

The lead dog warn't on a leash and were 'bout a mile 'way. The Blue Tick dog tried to git 'way. So they turned 'im loose. Now they had 'nother race started.

Them dogs went through a swamp bayhead, but we walked 'round. We seen 'em dogs goin' northeast. They turned back to Twin Lake, then the dogs bayed at a big ole oak.

Jack were walkin' 'round that big ole oak and we seen 'im jump and then grab 'is pistol. He shot 'bout 10 times.

We walked over where Jack were. They were a big ole rattle-snake.

The dogs had been 'round that tree, so we looked up and seen 2 coons. Byron quickly shot both of 'em.

Three coons could ruin a bunch of watermelons.

We leashed up the dogs but couldn't find one. So we looked all 'round and seen 'nother rattlesnake. So Byron kilt 'im.

We still hadn't found the other dog. We looked eve'where. Then Jack found 'im. The snake had bit 'im on the nose and he were dead.

I thank that snake coiled and the dog smelt 'im. Then the snake struck 'im. That's what I thank.

It were a real good hunt. Sorry the dog got kilt, but sometimes it

Skeeters and Hogs and Mules, Oh My!

happens.

We all went home. I shore were tired.

Jist 'bout ever'body hunted coon in watermelon season.
Red Fussell

A bayhead is a swamp habitat and can be found in margins of creeks with little or no creek banks.

Raccoon in Hackberry   *Peg Urban*

Too Quiet

Chapter 40

It were Friday after school. When we got off the bus we noticed they was no one settin' 'round Mr. Hall's store. We asked a black man what were goin' on, and he told us he warn't shore, but they was a bunch of people walkin' 'round Okahumpka. They was carryin' guns and they had badges. If'n y'all asked them somethang, they jist look at y'all.

Pretty soon some of 'em came by. We heerd one of them call the lady "Peg" and she called 'im "Hal". The rest didn't say nothang.

They looked behind ever'body's house, in they's barns, and all over by the creek. They asked Byron and me if'an we'd take 'em into the swamp. Mr. Hall had told 'em that we knowed the swamp best. And we sed we'd do it.

We asked what they was lookin' for. They sed, "A still."

I looked at Byron and he looked at me. We didn't want 'em to git caught.

We taked them to Lake Dunham Swamp and walked them in on the log. We told Mr. Hal, "Don't tell nobody 'bout this here log."

We showed 'em our treehouse, and they wanted to know what the trail were.

We sed, "That's where the gators crawl. We won't go out there 'cause

Skeeters and Hogs and Mules, Oh My!

they's a big gator out there."

We walked to Cason Hammock. They looked 'round in the swamp. They didn't even find a smell. So we walked over to Bugg Spring Run. Y'all could see Peg smellin' the air.

Then we walked to they's car. They gave us a soda water and a pack of crackers, and they thanked us.

They left and we walked back to Byron's house. His dad were outside and telled us they moved the still when they seen 'em people.

We telled Byron's dad that they left Okahumpka and we shore was glad.

They was 2 stills that I knowed of.

Red Fussell

Frog Huntin'

Chapter 41

Sunday night at church we talked 'bout goin' frog huntin'. We didn't have no frog gig though, so I asked my dad if'n he'd buy us 2 frog gigs.

He sed, "No. But y'all can build y'all's own."

They were an old car seat in the trash. It'd make a good one. I cut the springs up with a hack saw. The pieces was 'bout 12 inches, bent. We flattened the end and put it in the vice and filed a sharp point on the end.

My dad cut me 5 wedges and wrapped them with bailin' wire. We pulled the wire tight. It had 5 prongs. Byron were there so I gived that one to 'im, and he left to git 'is prunin' saw. Then he went to Bugg Spring to cut 2 bamboo poles.

While he were gone I cut out 'nother set and flattened the end on the anvil to sharpen the end and bent the gig. We used the pieces my dad made. They looked purdy good.

I got us a flour sack to keep the frogs in, and my dad had a head-light. But I had to go buy a battery for it.

Byron got a light from 'is Uncle Kocker. He had a good battery in 'is. I didn't asked if'n he asked 'is Uncle Kocker if'n he could use it.

Skeeters and Hogs and Mules, Oh My!

When I left the house, my mama told me to bring some home, but to clean 'em first. I didn't mind cleanin' frogs.

We went to Knowles pasture. Y'all can find lots of frogs there, but lots of snakes there too. They eat the frogs.

It were hard huntin' in that-there here pond. It had bushes all 'round it, but they shore was lots of frogs. We was giggin' and had a lot in the sack.

All of a sudden I bumped into somethang big! It scared me. It were jist a cow! They was several of 'em. I guess they seen the light and come to it.

They followed us all 'round that-there pond. When we left, they followed us to the fence. We climbed through the fence and started down the road.

Sy pulled up and wanted to know what we was doin'. He were a cowboy. We told 'im we was jist giggin'.

He sed, "I'll take the frogs."

I told Byron not to give 'im the frogs. And we told 'im we warn't gonna give 'im our frogs.

So he jist got in 'is car and drived off.

I asked Byron, "What do y'all thank he's gonna do?"

We never did hear nothang 'bout it 'gain, and we shore was glad.

We cleaned them frogs and throwed they's heads in the ditch. Some snakes will come by and eat 'em.

My mama cooked 'em frog legs. They don't jump out of the pan, but they shore do move in the pan!

To y'all who never eat frog legs afore, y'all should try 'em.
Red Fussell

A Frog Gig   *Sandy Kruse*
Red made this gig.

Cold Night

Chapter 42

They was a cold snap come in one day, so we covered the watermelon plants with paper and put dirt on the bottom of the paper so the air couldn't git to the plants. We started the day 'bout daylight.

It shore were gittin' colder, but we knowed we didn't wanta quit. It had-a be did today. When we finished the field it were almost dark.

Mr. Willis come by as we was leavin'. He told us he needed someone help to fire 'is orange grove.

So my dad sed, "Boys, he needs some help."

So Byron and me et supper and put on some warm clothes at our house. Mr. Willis had smudge pots. We put kerosene with some gas to git the generator started and fired the pots with a fire starter. It put out a black smoke.

I shore were tired, but this hada be did or 'is grove'd freeze. When we had all the fires goin', we laid up in the haystack where it were warm. I laid down and went right to sleep. A little later he woke us up to fire up the smudge pots 'gain. The wind picked up now and it were real cold.

Mr. Willis hoped the wind would keep blowin' to keep the frost off the trees. We had all the smudge pots on fire 'gain, so we hit the hay

James Carlton Fussell

'gain where it were warm. Then one of 'em smudge pots blowed up. I guess it had too much gas in it.

Mr. Willis had an extra one, so we fired it up. The smoke were real bad, but that keeps the trees from freezin'.

We headed to the hay stack, and it shore felt good.

Then 'bout daylight, Mr. Willis woke us up to fill the pots and set the fires 'gain. 'Bout 6 or 7 o'clock would be the worst time. I don't know why.

He come back and brought somethang to eat and made some coffee. It shore felt good in our stomachs.

The sun come up. It were still cold, but in 'bout an hour we could turn off the smudge pots and close the lids to save the fuel. I were ready to go home.

Then my dad come by and told us we'd have to take the paper off the watermelon plants. I telled 'im, "I jist don't thank I could do it. I'm so tired."

So he telled us to go on home and take the paper off when it started to warm up.

Byron went home and I went home, washed my face and hands and feet and laid down in that feather bed.

My mama woke me up later and telled me it were supper time and she needed some wood for the stove.

So I chopped wood for the stove in the kitchen and the fireplace. We shore do burn a lot of wood. The fireplace jist gits you warm on one side.

Most of the time we built us a fire where the wind didn't blow on us outside.

We saved the watermelon field and the orange grove. Mr. Willis asked us what he owed us, but we jist telled 'im, "Nothang."

He still tried to pay us, but we wouldn't take nothang.

At this time in my life, I learnt that we had-a
help people in need.
That stuck with me all my life.
Red Fussell

132

Hog Killin'

Chapter 43

When cold weather come 'round, it were hog killin' time. My dad butchered anybody's hog for them, if'n they asked. He done it jist for a rear ham. They cooked the outside of the hog to draw the grease out of the pork rind and saved the belly for bacon.

They was always plenty of people to help. My mama fixed a big dinner and people would brang some food. They'd even git ice to have tea.

We didn't have no place to put the meat on ice, so they put it in the smokehouse and fired it up with hickory wood and leaves and nuts. It takes days to dry out the meat, and it were real hot in the smoke house.

My dad had a bucket of honey and dipped the ham in the bucket ever'day 'til it were dried out. And he smoked the bacon. MMM! I shore did like it. Y'all could smell it for days. And he gived the dog some scraps. That dog shore were a good watch dog, but he showed ever'body where we had some stuff hid.

My dad would say, "Here comes the preacher. Hide the cake."

We all laffed.

Hog killin' day were hard work, but my dad seemed to like it. He were good at what he done. And if'n someone needed somethang, he'd give it to them, even if'n he needed it. He taught us a lot 'bout life.

I watched 'im skin a goat for the man at Helena Run one day. He telled me to never git any hair on the meat. It would ruin it.

All this stuff was hard work, but we done it jist to git by. The ole house we lived in were nothin' to look at, but I warn't never 'shamed of it.

My dad taught me to always do my best and not to worry 'bout the rest.

Both my dad and my brother liked to eat. They'd eat 'bout anythang, 'cept my brother wouldn't eat coon. Not even if'n I brought it home already cleaned.

The nights was cold in the ole house, but if'n y'all got in the feather bed y'all'd be warm in jist a few minutes. 'Course it were cold when y'all got up and y'all's clothes was cold. But they'd warm up in the kitchen by the wood stove.

I 'member my mama heatin' water and gived me a cup of hot water jist to warm up.

The chickens fluffed they's feathers to stay warm. In a wind storm, I always wondered how chickens stayed on a limb. But Mr. Mike telled me they lock they's feet when they set down. I did notice that when it's cold, them chickens don't lay as good neither.

I 'member my mama havin' a quiltin' party. Ever'body saved they's scraps of flour sacks when they sewed stuff, and then a bunch of ladies'd all sew 'em together while they talked, to make a quilt. When they was through, that quilt shore felt good on a cold night. And it were purdy too.

My mama's hair turned gray at a young age.
I guess I mighta did that.
Red Fussell

Skeeters and Hogs and Mules, Oh My!

Hog Pen

A Jug of 'Shine

Chapter 44

When we got off the bus they was all kinds of people standin' 'round. They was talkin' to ever'body and one man pointed at us. He asked if'n we knowed Miss Sanders.

We told 'im, "Yes."

Then he wanted to know if'n she won any money shootin'.

We told 'im, "She shore did. She won 450 dollars. Why?"

He told us he'd ask the questions.

So I told Byron that we wouldn't tell 'im anythang more then.

He sed, "Y'all either tell me what I wanta know or y'all can go to jail. Now, where is the still?"

We told 'im we didn't know.

So he put us in the back seat of 'is car. The door warn't locked so we left and hid under the depot. We seen 'is car go by, but he didn't stop.

I told Byron, "I'm goin' home." And I did.

My mama wanted to know what were goin' on.

I told 'er, "I don't know."

A man drove up in our yard and he asked my mama if'n I were home. She sed, "Yes. What do y'all want with 'im?"

He sed he'd ask the questions. So she telled 'im to git goin' then.

Skeeters and Hogs and Mules, Oh My!

I don't thank he liked that. My dad come in from the field and wanted to know what were wrong. My mama telled 'im what the man sed and that she telled 'im to "Git".

We looked outside and they was 3 cars out front. They knocked on the side of the house and wanted to see me.

My dad telled me to come to the door, and then the men telled me, "We jist bought a gallon of shine from Miss Sanders' son, and we thank y'all knows where the still are."

I telled them, "I know where they's still are. They moved it when Hal and Peg come lookin' 'round 'bout a month a go. I can show y'all where it were."

They sed, 'Ok."

So we went to Sutton Landing in the Quarters. We had to walk part of the way. Peg and Hal was there and Peg sed, "I do smell a still. When we got here they had poured out the mash and the hogs had been in it. But it still smelled rotten."

The man sed, "Who runs the still?"

I telled 'im, "I don't know."

He sed, "Boy, I'll put y'all in jail."

My dad jist looked at 'im and telled me to go on home.

The man sed, "I'll tell y'all when y'all can go home."

But we jist walked off. He hollered at us. My dad looked at me and sed, "I thank he's mad." We kept walkin' and walked through the woods.

When we got home they was there 'gain. The man started to say somethang but my dad telled 'im to shut 'is mouth and to git!

Then they went back to Miss Sanders', so we went too. They was 'bout 20 people standin' there. They was lookin' for shine and had a jug.

Miss Sanders asked if'n she could see the jug of shine, so they handed it to her. She dropped it on a rock and it broke.

Now I've seen mad people afore, but not as mad as he were. He started to grab Miss Sanders by the shoulders, but a bystander telled 'im not to. He looked at the crowd and knowed he better not do that.

They put 'er in 'is car and then started lookin' for more shine. They had a piece of steel rod they pushed in the ground 'bout ever' 6 inches. They was 10 of 'em doin' it. One sed, "I hit somethang."

I thought, *I shore hope not.*

They started diggin' down, but it were Mr. Knight's trash pile. Then they walked 'cross the road, and they was a trail to a spring.

I telled the man, "We go over there and take a bath."

He looked at me real funny.

They walked out in the swamp, but it were full of snakes. Peg sed, "I don't smell nothang here."

They went back to the house. They even looked in the outhouse. I'd hate to know I drank somethang that come out of the outhouse!

They spent all day lookin' at 'er place and part of the woods. All they found were trash. They looked in the cane patch and under the house.

The car Miss Sanders was in were hot! I opened the door so it would be a little cooler.

Miss Sanders asked me if'n they found anythang 'cross the road, but I telled 'er, "No."

They was 4 men lookin' all week. They looked 'gain all over the house and even went back to the spring. Then they walked down to the edge of the swamp 'gain.

When that jug were busted they didn't have no case, so they jist telled 'em they would stay in touch. Then they let Miss Sanders out of the car.

I knowed they must be a still in the swamp, but it must be where they's lots of snakes.

All them revenuers finally left and we went home.

I were settin' on the porch with my dad and I asked 'im, "Is there a still in the swamp?"

He jist laffed. Sed, "It's not in the swamp. The still is by Sutton Landing. He moved it when Hal and Peg first come."

I sed, "Where does he keep the shine?"

He laffed 'gain and sed, "They built 2 boxes in the out house. Y'all hada raise the seat. It were down tight. Y'all hada remove 2 pegs to raise the seat, but don't tell nobody. Sellin' shine is what they live on. But then, y'all know if'n y'all turn 'er in y'all git 50 dollars."

I'd never turn 'er in for money. We liked 'er.

The next shine y'all drink may have come
from Miss Sander's outhouse!
Red Fussell

A Night on Bugg Spring Run

Chapter 45

It were a hot Friday night. We talked 'bout goin' out on Bugg Spring Run. The wind were mild. So 'bout 8 o'clock we went. The skeeters warn't so bad then.

We cut some flat lighter splinters to go on the front of the boat. We taked an old .22 gun that Byron's Uncle Kocker had. We never shot it, but we'd need somethang to kill snakes. In warm weather snakes is bad. And we had a piece of wire we got off a bale of hay.

We was tryin' to catch a soft shell turtle. Them alligator turtles ain't as good as the soft shell turtles.

We put the boat out at Cason Hammock. I were pushin' the boat. We jist knowed someone were watchin' us. Byron looked at me and he pointed where he thought he were.

Then Byron sed, "Who's there?"

Nobody answered. So I told Byron to shoot that direction and he'd answer!

Finally a man sed, "I'm here. Where 'yall boys goin'?"

Byron told 'im, "To catch a soft shell turtle."

He sed, "Y'all got a gun?"

We sed, "Yes."

Then he wanted to know if'n we was gator huntin'. But we telled 'im we warn't.

We paddled off. We knowed who he were. He were the game warden. They say Ed, that's 'is name, would put 'is mother in jail. He telled us to come back to shore, but we jist paddled on.

We seen some turtles but most of 'em was small. Then Byron seen the biggest gar fish! We eased up on 'im and Byron put a loop over 'is head and snatched it up. That fish got mad and we went 'round and 'round.

Byron were holdin' 'im and I were tryin' to keep the boat out of the bushes but I warn't doin' a good job of it. The gar fish were tryin' to bite Byron and he jumped at 'im.

I were thinkin', maybe we should jist let 'im go.

He come by the boat bitin' ever'thang in sight. Finally, he gived out and I telled Byron, "I'm not shore I want 'im in the boat."

But Byron wired 'is mouth shut and we finally got 'im in the boat. It were 'bout as long as the boat!

We started back down the run and Byron seen a big alligator turtle. But we let 'im go on. They warn't any big soft shell turtles out tonight.

I telled Byron, "I'll bet Ed's still there!"

Byron sed, "We ain't breakin' the law."

I sed, "We have that-there gun."

So we pulled over and put it in a tree fork, jist in case. We'd pick it back up on Saturday.

When we paddled up to the bank, there were Ed. He sed, "Well, boys, I finally caught y'all."

I sed, "What for?"

He sed, "Y'all can't have a gun and a light at the same time in the woods at night."

I telled 'im, "We ain't got no gun."

He sed, "Yes, y'all do. I seen it."

We asked 'im where he seen it and he looked in the bottom of the boat. When he didn't find it he wanted to know what we done with it.

We jist looked at 'im. He telled us, "Some day I'll git y'all!"

Skeeters and Hogs and Mules, Oh My!

We telled 'im, "Bye."

We carried that gar fish home. We want to show our mamas what we catched.

> We did catch a big gar fish.
> It had a bad mouth.
> Red Fussell

A Gar Fish

Soft-shell Turtle

Possum

Chapter 46

I had an old red-bone hound. He were good for nothin' but he'd foller me ever'where I'd go.

RH had a dog of all kinds. It would catch possums. So we'd catch possums and gived 'em to Jack. Jack lived with Miss Abby in a little house. They'd eat or sell them possums.

RH's dog would put one up a persimmon tree. We'd push 'im out with a stick and git 'im in a sack. Then we'd give 'im to Jack.

One day, Byron's little brother, Larry sed, "Why don't y'all dye 'im green like y'all done that mule?"

Well, we still had some dye left. So we telled Larry to hold 'im while we dyed 'im. We dyed ever'thang but 'is head.

Most possums is a dirty white. We taked the now-green possum back to the edge of the swamp, and caught 'bout 10 more possums. We dyed 'em all green, and we let 'em all go. Larry's arms was green too.

If'n anyone wanted to know who dyed them possums, we'd jist tell 'em to look at Larry.

When the snake man were huntin' he seen a green possum and were tellin' people 'bout it, but they'd look at 'im as if to say, "That ain't true."

Skeeters and Hogs and Mules, Oh My!

Then ever'time we'd find a gofer, we'd dye 'im. And anythang else we could catch, we'd dye 'em.

We told our school teacher they's green possums in the edge of the swamp. So she told 'er husband and he wanted to see one.

They come out one night. We got RH's dog and we hunted a while. We was 'bout to give up when the dog treed a green possum. The teacher's husband had 'is camera and taked 'is picture. Nobody'd ever seen a green possum. He sent the picture somewhere, and they sed that possum must be sick.

The was a bunch come out to see the green possums. I telled Byron, "I thank we'd better leave."

But Byron sed, "We've gone too far. I don't thank we can git out of it."

People was comin' from school in a big school bus. They had all kinds of cameras with poles to set they's cameras on.

We taked RH's dog next to the swamp and hunted 'bout an hour. Then the dog treed one, but it warn't a possum. I smelled 'im first. It were a pole cat!

I telled Byron, "Do y'all 'member when we got sprayed? I don't want no more of that."

The bunch of people was headin' straight toward that pole cat. The dog got sprayed 'cause he got too close, and then he rubbed on some of the people. They thought it were funny, but they didn't know it wouldn't wash off.

When they got on the bus, it smelt like that pole cat! I don't thank they wanted to see no more possums. They had 'bout all they could stand.

We watched the bus leave. The teacher's husband looked at us and jist laffed. But he smelt like the pole cat too, 'cause the dog done rubbed up 'gainst 'im.

He sed, "I thank I seen all the green possums I wanna see."

He went out in the pond behind Byron's house and tryed to wash the smell off. But it didn't come off.

The next day at school, even the teacher smelt like a pole cat. She sed, "Stay away from 'em boys."

I did make a passin' grade in this class
Red Fussell

Opossum

Jist Nothin' to Do

Chapter 47

We loaded up the wagon, hooked up Charley, and rode off to see Mr. Mike. We rode by the dairy and seen the man that owns the dairy. But we jist kept on goin'. We rode through the woods, then by the gun range and unloaded the mower. Then we hooked up Charley. I got the mower and mowed most of the grass and then Byron mowed. We raked the grass and loaded it in the wagon. Then we left. It didn't look like they'd been shootin'.

We crossed over to Mr. Mike's house and taked the mower off the wagon and mowed 'is yard and field. We raked most of the grass and put it in the wagon. He seen us and come outside. He wanted to know how much he owed us.

We jist told 'im, "Nothin.'"

Then Miss Sweetie Pie come out and she told us to wash our hands. She gived us a piece of pie—a big piece of pie—and one of them soda waters.

Mr. Mike asked us how Miss Sanders were doin'. We told 'im we hadn't been by. Then he asked 'bout the green possums. And he laffed. He sed, "I'll bet y'all boys dyed them possums."

We didn't say nothin'.

Then he sed, "And one of 'em men that were on that bus were my son, Daniel. He didn't smell good for 'bout a month. He don't wanna see no green possum. He told us that bus still don't smell no good. And when that bus got back to town, someone asked them all if'n they seen a green possum."

We still jist looked at 'im.

He sed, "I heard some of 'em even sed some bad words. And when Daniel got home 'is wife, Virginia, wouldn't even let 'im sleep in the house. So he hada sleep in the carport."

We still hadn't sed nothin'. We jist looked at 'im.

Mr. Mike sed, "I knowed when I heerd 'bout it that y'all boys had done dyed them possums."

We still jist looked at 'im and let 'im talk.

Mr. Mike sed, "I shore wish I coulda seen 'em possums."

We was through with our pie so told 'im we hada go home.

He thanked us for mowin'.

We like Mr. Mike and Miss Sweetie Pie. She hugged our necks.

If'n y'all' wanna see green possums, y'all should come to Okahumpka.
They may still be some.
Red Fussell

When We Got Back

Chapter 48

We unloaded the hay from the wagon and laid it out to dry. If'n y'all put it up wet, it could catch on fire or mold.

I sed, "Let's ride out to Miss Sanders."

We started out on the clay road and seen Bill and Larry and they's 2 brothers walkin'. Byron sed, "Wanna ride?"

Larry sed, "We ain't goin' to no mud hole, is we?"

We all laffed. They won't never forget that mud hole.

We told 'em we was goin' to Miss Sanders. They was goin' to the spring to cool off.

Ole Charley warn't fast, but we was ridin' and not walkin'. Ever' once in a while I thank 'bout the man that gived us Charley. We've shore had some good times with 'im.

We got to Miss Sanders and she were settin' on the porch in a rockin' chair. We knowed she were dippin' snuff. She asked us if'n we'd like a cigar.

We sed, "Shore."

We lit them cigars up and smoked them down. Then we got a handful of camphor leaves to chew to kill the smell and the taste.

Miss Sanders sed, "Thank y'all for helpin' me when them revenuers come. They jist 'bout got our still. But it's hid good now."

We telled 'er we hadda leave so we'd be home afore dark.

We started home, picked up Bill and Larry and the other 2 boys. They hopped on the back of the wagon.

Bill telled us when they got home from the mud puddle, they's mama put a good whippin' on 'em. Sed they wouldn't forget that one for a while, and she telled them to stay out of the mud! She sed, "If'n I catch 'yall doin' it 'gain, I'll beat the tar out of y'all."

We all laffed.

They got out at Byron's house 'cause they hadda be home afore their mama were lookin' for 'em.

I don't thank we'll ever forget that mud hole. It were fun!
Red Fussell

Leaves on a Camphor Tree   *Peg Urban*

Flyin' Squirrel

Chapter 49

We was swingin' on the swing. They was a bunch of us. We seen a squirrel glidin' from tree to tree and thought it'd make a nice pet. All we hadda do were to catch 'im. Well, I knowed if'n y'all catched 'im he'd be full of teeth and try to bite us.

We sed if'n we got a wire basket and put it over the hole in the tree, he'd go in. We was gonna smoke 'im out of the tree 'cause they's a hole at the bottom of the tree too. We built a little fire at the bottom and put leaves on it, and he'd come out into our wire basket.

Well, that's the way it should work. But ever'thang don't work like it should.

We went home to git what we needed to do this and come back. We built the fire and put the leaves on it. Byron were on a ladder holdin' the cage. RH were buildin' the fire at the bottom of the tree, and smoke started comin' out the hole up by Byron. The squirrel didn't come to the cage, but snakes did!

Byron had 3 big snakes in the cage and he dropped it. He were still standin' on the ladder and then that flyin' squirrel come out and landed right on Byron's head,

I sed, "Catch 'im!"

James Carlton Fussell

Byron sed, "Y'all catch 'im!"

That squirrel then run up the tree, turned 'round and looked at us.

With all the excitement with the squirrel, we wasn't payin' no 'tention to the fire. By then the whole oak tree were on fire.

Byron sed, "Jist let it burn down!" And it did.

Melba sed, "Now that squirrel don't got no place to live." And she were real mad.

Melba is another of Byron's sisters in real life.
Red Fussell

Flying Squirrel   *Steve Gettle*

A Rough Night in the Swamp

Chapter 50

It were one of 'em dark nights. Y'all couldn't even see nothang. And we decided to spend the night in the swamp. They was lots of lightnin' and high winds. Jist a bad, bad night! Then it started hailin' and knock- in' leaves off the trees. We could see it hit the ground from our tree house. I thought shore our house would fall, even though we nailed it real good.

I told Byron, "We shoulda stayed at home!"

But it were too late now. We couldn't leave. We was dry for now, but I didn't know for how long.

In the lightnin' I could see Ole Joe swimmin' by. He were jist lookin' for somethang to eat. Jist hope our tree house don't fall.

I told Byron, "We could go home in the rain, but the hail would hurt us." It were beatin' on the tin roof and sounded jist like some one were beatin' on the top of it with a hammer.

Byron sed, "Look, that looks like somebody down there."

Byron climbed down the tree and hollered at the man. The man an- swered 'im. He come to the tree where Byron were and then they both left. I didn't know what were goin' on.

I seen Byron cut a big cabbage plant fan and they went through the swamp.

Now that warn't a good thang to do!

In a few minutes he come back with a woman. She climbed up the ladder into the tree house with Byron and the other man. Now they was 4 of us up there and the wind were blowin' hard. She were shakin' from bein' so cold.

She taked off 'er wet clothes and wrapped up in the blanket. We had to wring out 'er clothes the best we could, but they was still wet.

The man told us they was on an air boat and the motor quit. They was gonna wait out the storm, but then it got real bad, and the boat sunk. They got under a cabbage palm tree. He left 'er there and telled 'er he were goin' for help.

Then he wanted to know what we was doin' out in the swamp.

We telled 'im, "We come down here quite a bit."

We wrung out 'is clothes too. We was so crowded I thought shore we was gonna fall out.

He put 'is clothes back on and wrapped up in Byron's blanket. I warn't all that cold, but they was wet and cold.

It were gonna be a long night. We all laid down and went to sleep.

When I waked up it were daylight and the sun were shinin'. Byron were buildin' a fire to dry 'em all out.

All we had to eat were 2 eggs and some pancake mix. Well, we cooked it and shared it with them 2 people. Then we put out the fire and walked out on the log, and walked down Stage Coach Road. They was water ever'where.

I asked Byron, "Should we go the clay road?"

We both thought that would be the best way. We walked to the store. They had a phone and the man could call someone to come and git 'em.

While they was talkin' on the phone, we left. I needed to git home.

When I got home, my dad asked me where we spent the night.

I telled 'im, "In the woods in our treehouse."

I telled 'im, "I woulda come home, but I felt safer to stay put." He agreed.

Then 'bout a week later, a man stopped by the house. I didn't know who he were. His wife were a nice lookin' lady. They sed they was the ones in the swamp.

When I seen 'im in the swamp, he looked like a drown'd rat!

They bought us 2 sleepin' bags, and they was waterproof. And they bought us a pair of nice boots with a huntin' knife. Then we all went to Byron's to show 'im what 'em people gave us. We thanked 'em, and they thanked us. They sed we saved they's lives.

Then the man sed, "Y'all know that log y'all walked out on. Does ever'body know 'bout it?"

We told 'im, "No, and we don't want y'all to tell nobody 'bout it neither. They's 'bout 4 feet of mud there if'n y'all don't use the log."

The man sed, "If'n y'all hadn't seen us, I doubt we coulda waded out."

They thanked us 'gain and we taked our new sleepin' bags out to the tree house. Our house were still there and didn't git blowed down.

Them sleepin' bags would sleep better than the grass mattress we made. When we opened up the bags in the tree house, they was a pair of gloves too, and a thank you note!

We spent lots of nights in the swamp
but not as bad as that night.
Red Fussell

James Carlton Fussell

A Tree House

Skeeters and Hogs and Mules,
Oh My!

A Good Day

Chapter 51

It were Friday and I were walkin' home from Mr. Hall's store. The man in the swamp drived up and asked me if'n Byron and me would like to go on an airplane ride.

So he drived me over to Byron's house and Byron come outside. The man sed, "I'm gonna fly to Tampa. Would y'all wanta fly down with me?"

We sed, "Shore!"

He told us he'd pick us up Saturday mornin'.

Well, I were so excited I didn't sleep. I were really lookin' forward to it. I ain't never flyed in an airplane.

His wife picked us up and we rode to the airport. The man told us to fasten our seat belts. Then he revved up the motor, and we was off the ground.

He sed, "Look out the window. Can y'all see y'all's tree house?"

We shore could! Then he got real high and we could see all the lakes. I didn't know it looked like that.

It didn't take long and we was in Tampa. He told us he had a business meetin', so he left us with 'is wife. She hired a taxi and we went into Tampa and rode on a street car. Them thangs make lots of noise.

We went where they rolled cigars. I told Byron, "We need to find out how much they cost." We had 2 dollars.

We asked the lady rollin' them cigars and telled 'er we had a friend, Miss Sanders, who smoked 'em. She had a box full and they was some that warn't rolled right. They still smoked. We asked 'er how much for a box for our friend.

She sed, "For y'all's friend – free."

We hugged 'er neck. We was so happy.

We left and went back to the airport. The man were still in a meetin'. So the lady bought us a Cuban sandwich. I never had one of them afore, but it were real good.

When we got back on the plane, the man asked what were in the box.

We telled 'im, "Cigars for Miss Sanders".

He looked at them and then he sed, "Wait a minute."

He made a phone call, and here come a man out to the plane. He handed 'im a box and he put it on the plane. Then he started the engine and we was off the ground. I shore liked that.

It didn't take long and we was back in Leesburg.

We telled 'im, "We shore had a good time."

When we started to leave he handed me the box. It were full of cigars.

He sed, "These are good cigars for Miss Sanders."

When we got to Okahumpka the man's wife sed, "Where does Miss Sanders live?"

We telled 'er. So they drived us to Miss Sanders' house and we gived 'er all the cigars.

She didn't know what to say.

We telled Miss Sanders who gived them to us.

She thanked us all and then sed, "When y'all want one, come on by."

The man's wife heered 'er, and she jist smiled.

I got out at Byron's house, and we thanked them for flyin' us to Tampa.

They sed, "We'll do it 'gain sometime."

But we never seen them 'gain. We didn't even know they's names.

We helped Miss Sanders smoke them cigars.
Red Fussell

Skeeters and Hogs and Mules,
Oh My!

Piper Cub tail dragger

James Carlton Fussell

Somebody New

Chapter 52

They's a new family moved south of Red Hill Grove. Ed and Peg was they's names. They sed he were in the Navy, so that's why he wared one them Navy hats. They moved to the ole Snyder place. It were a big farm with some good farm land.

They put up a fence like I never seen afore. We counted 'em strings of bob wire. It were 8 feet high and ever' 6 inches they was a piece of bob wire. The posts was 5 feet apart. So y'all couldn't crawl through 'em.

They was posted signs to keep out on ever' post. I thank they was serious about us stayin' out.

We heered 'is wife were a parole officer too, and that she were bad when someone made 'er mad. If'n a guy got out of jail early, he'd have to go see 'er.

If'n Mrs. Peg told 'em to set down and they didn't do it, one of 'er big boys knocked 'em down. They didn't have to be knocked down more'n once.

I hear tell that if'n them that were let out of jail didn't do right, Mrs. Peg sed she'd put one of 'em balls big as a bowling ball with a chain on they's leg and put 'em on the farm. If'n they didn't work, they'd only git bread and water and they'd sleep on the floor.

It didn't take long afore they went to work. And when she turned 'em loose, they didn't wanna git in no more trouble.

She wouldn't tell no one what her address were neither. She'd blindfold 'em jist out of jail when they come out and 'gain when they left.

I told Byron, "I shore don't wanna go to no jail and wind up on 'er farm.

They needed a new road down 'er way so she called a company that done roads. She were told they'd send a man out to check it out.

Well, they send one of 'em men that had been sent to 'er farm to work after jail. He told 'er that he'd never come back there.

Ed and Peg worked the farm for 'bout 10 years. Then they sold it and moved to town.

Some of the people that stayed at the farm sed they learned how to farm and how to keep they's mouth shut!

It kept a lot of people from goin' back to jail.

The law left 'er alone. She were doin' such a good job.

This Peg ain't a revenuer. This Peg were a parole officer.
Red Fussell

Jist for the Fun of It

Chapter 53

Saturday rolled 'round. We loaded the wagon with hay and hooked Charley up. Betty Jean wanted to know where we was goin'. We told her, "Jist for a ride."

She wanted to go, but sed she hadda wash the dishes. Byron told 'er we'd pick 'er up on the way back.

We rode out to Red Hill Grove and asked that red-head girl if'n she'd like to go for a ride. Ruth were there too, and she wanted to know if'n she could go.

We sed, "Shore."

They climbed up in the wagon and we left. We stopped at Miss Sanders. She were settin' out on the porch. We asked 'er if'n we could have a cigar. She tried to give us one out of the box, but we told 'er to give one out of the bag.

I really wanted to see that red-headed girl light one up.

She done it. She taked a drag, and then she throwed that thang down and coffed and coffed. I picked it up and smoked it.

Ruth lit 'er's and sed she liked it.

Byron were smokin' 'is too.

We stayed there for 'bout an hour. Miss Sanders sed 'er son were

Skeeters and Hogs and Mules, Oh My!

workin'.

I didn't say nothin', but I'd bet he were runnin' that still.

I didn't know where the still were, but I knowed I wouldn't drink nothin' out of no outhouse.

We told Miss Sanders we needed to git goin'.

We got us some camphor leaves and chewed 'em to git rid of the smell.

We went by the snake man's house. RH were there and wanted to know where we was goin'.

We told 'im we was jist takin' a ride, and to jump on the wagon. Then we stopped at Byron's house. Betty Jean were done with the dishes. Her little brother, Larry wanted to go. So we told 'im to climb on,

We went down the clay road to Mr. Hall's store. We bought 3 Black Cow candy bars. That's what we'd have for lunch. As we was leavin', here come Larry and Bill. We asked 'em if'n they want to go.

They sed they'd have to ask they's mama. So we rode to they's house and she come out. They asked if'n they could ride with us.

She sed, "Y'all can go as long as they ain't no mud hole!"

Then we went by the depot and Barbara and Joanne was throwin' rocks at the railroad sign. We asked if'n they wanted to go for a ride on the wagon.

So they climbed in. We had a wagon full. Poor Charley.

We rode by the dairy where they was milkin' the cows. We crossed the road and taked the long way 'round. Then we crossed over by the island.

I told Byron, "I smell that still. Do y'all?"

He sed, "Shore do." But we didn't say nothang.

The bunch in the wagon started singin'. I thank Charley like it too. I telled Byron that Charley kept time with 'is tail. We jist laffed.

We crossed the ditches. They were a bad sand bed. Ever'body got off so Charley could go through it easier. Then they all climbed back on. Afore we started back up, Byron broke them Black Cow candy bars and gived ever'body some. That were lunch.

We rode to Col. Keith's house. He were outside and stopped what he were doin' to talk to us.

He sed, "Thank y'all for mowin' the gun range." And he telled us he

161

might open it up some time.

His wife come out and told us to wait a minute. Then she brought out a big box of cookies and gived ever'body one. I asked 'er if'n Charley could have one too.

She sed, "Shore." And she gived Charley one. He licked 'is lips.

We thanked 'er for the cookies and ever'one started singin' 'gain as we left.

We crossed over the highway. Charley didn't like the cars, so we tried to keep 'im on the dirt road. We stopped at Mr. Mike's house. He were settin' on the porch.

When we rode up, we all got off the wagon. Mr. Mike got a bucket and gived Charley some water and some corn. Charley shore did like that.

Then Miss Sweetie Pie told the girls to come and help 'er bake a quick cake. Mr. Mike made some lemonade. It didn't take 'em long and we all had some.

We thanked 'em and loaded up to start home. I knowed Charley would be glad when we got home.

It'd been a fun day.

RH got off at the store and so did Larry and Bill. We stopped at Byron's house and Betty Jean and Larry got off. Then we rode out to Red Hill Grove and the girls got off. They sed they had a good time.

We come back to Byron's house, fed Charley, wiped 'im down and he rolled in the dirt.

Camphor Tree   *Peg Urban*

The Fire

Chapter 54

We was settin' at the depot watchin' the trains go by. I asked Byron, "Look, does that train have a hot box?"

We both looked. Ashes was fallin' out the engine. We looked down the track and the grass were on fire too.

We ran in and told the agent what we seen. He got on the machine that clicks and told Center Hill what we seen. I went on home.

Later, the law come out to Okahumpka to check on the fire. They was fire all down the railroad tracks. The sheriff comed out to our house and told me a woman told 'im that she seen Byron and me settin' the fires. Them fires went all the way to Center Hill and started someplace in Leesburg.

I told the sheriff we seen the train loosing ashes that was on fire.

He had Byron in the back of 'is car and put me in 'is car too. I told Byron, "That crazy old woman sed we set them fires!"

We told the sheriff to ask the agent what we seen. So the sheriff drived us to the agent's house. The agent come outside and the sheriff talked to 'im. When he come back, he headed to our houses to drop us off.

When we got out, we asked the sheriff, "What did he say?"

James Carlton Fussell

The sheriff sed, "Not much."

Well, my dad got in 'is truck and had Byron and me git in. He taked us to Tavares to the sheriff's office. He talked to the the high sheriff 'bout what happened.

They called the sheriff in that accused us. When it were over, the sheriff had us go outside. He sed, "I'm sorry I accused y'all." And he really looked like he were sorry too. He went on to tell us he were gonna go after the woman that sed we done it.

I telled Byron, "We should string 'er house!"

I don't know what they fined 'er, but she shaked 'er fist at us.

We did enough stuff to go to jail, but we didn't set that fire.
Red Fussell

Settin' at Mr. Hall's Store

Chapter 55

We'd go and set at Mr. Hall's store, and sometimes we could git a job. Well, up drived the man that we pulled Maypop for. He asked if'n we'd like a job.

We sed, "Shore."

He sed, "I'll pick y'all up in the mornin' 'bout 7 here at the store."

The next mornin' we climbed in 'is truck and went on the back side of Bridges Road. They was a bunch of Maypops back there in them woods. It shore were hot!

I bringed a jug of water and sweet taters, and had a feed sack wrapped 'round it to keep it cool. Then I put it in the shade.

He had a real big trailer. We pulled Maypops 'bout all mornin'. At lunch time he told us to keep pullin' Maypops, and that he'd be back in a little while.

We did stop and eat sweet taters that I bringed and drinked 'bout all the water. I told Byron, "I don't thank he's comin' back."

Well, 'bout 4 o'clock we left. It'd be a real long walk home. We walked out on the highway and a man picked us up. We told 'im what we was doin'.

He sed, "Somethang must-a happened to 'im."

James Carlton Fussell

When I got home my mama asked why we was so late. I telled 'er that the man left at noon and didn't come back for us.

The next day he come to pick us up. I warn't shore I wanted to go back.

He sed, "I'm sorry. I got drunk and forgot all 'bout y'all."

Byron sed, "Let's go back. He always pays us."

So we went. We worked 'til 'bout noon and loaded all y'all could put on a truck and trailer. We started to leave, when this strange man come up.

He sed, "Them's my Maypops."

He sed he owned the land. We jist looked at the man we worked for.

The man we worked for sed, "We're not gonna unload them. You don't own this-here land. I know who does."

The man reached for somethang in 'is truck, but he didn't make it. The man we worked for slammed the door on 'is arm.

The man we worked for reached for 'is gun. I thought shore he were gonna shoot the strange man. Well, he didn't shoot 'im, but he taked the stranger's gun off the seat in the truck and put the barrel of the gun in a fork of a tree. Then he bent the barrel so that it would shoot 'round a corner.

I heered 'im tell that stranger, "Y'all can bluff some people, but not me! So the best thang y'all can do is leave now!"

The man left, but I don't thank he were too happy.

We was ridin' down the road and seem 'im. He raised a pistol and shot at the truck we was in.

The man we worked for stopped the truck and jumped out with 'is shot gun. The stranger ran down the road and through the woods.

We went on then to Umatilla and sold the Maypop. Then the man bringed us back to Okahumpka and he gived us 5 dollars each.

We telled 'im he paid us too much, but he sed, "No. If'n I need y'all boys, I'll let y'all know."

Then 'bout a week later they were a shoot out in Oxford. One man were killed, but it warn't the man we knowed.

Maypops ain't bad to eat but have lots of seeds.
Red Fussell

We're Cookin'

Chapter 56

We made a trip in the swamp lookin' for somethang to cook. We didn't find nothin'. We'd been there almost all day. It jist seemed like ever'thang left the swamp.

So we headed over to the swamp where our treehouse were. We waded in on the log, climbed up in the treehouse, rolled out our sleepin' bags and checked for scorpions. Them thangs hurt when they sting y'all.

We laid up there for 'bout an hour and then Old Joe, the gator come by. I told Byron, "Let 'im go."

We seen the bushes shakin' and we both got ready. That big ole hog come out. I told Byron, "All that big ole hog would do is stink up the woods!"

Y'all could see where we shot 'is ears. We jist let 'im go.

Later Byron shaked me and sed, "Look, they's a small gator that swimmed out."

I shot 'im and he rolled. Well, when he rolled 'nother gator grabbed 'im. I raised to shoot 'gain, but they was gone. I ain't never seen anythang so quick!

As we laid there we looked down and we both laffed. Y'all'd never guess what we seen. It were 'bout as funny as I ever seen.

I warn't gonna tell y'all what it were, but I will. It were green! It were one of them possums we dyed green.

Wonder if'n them people that comed to see the green possums and met that pole cat seen this one.

I asked Byron, "Wanna eat a green possum?"

He sed, "No! No tellin' what he et."

We still hadn't seen nothang but that gator. So we left and went to Cason Hammock. There we seen a swamp rabbit. Byron kilt 'im and we looked 'round and kilt 3 more.

So we taked them to the hog pen and skinned 'em. Then we put 'em in flour and put some lard in the pan. Larry and Betty Jean showed up. We fried 'em rabbits.

Now we never et no swamp rabbit afore, but didn't know why we couldn't.

After we fried 'em we laid 'em on a piece of tin and telled Larry to git a piece. He chomped down and then spit it out. We asked 'im what were wrong.

He sed, "Tastes like mud!"

We got a piece too, and he were right. It warn't fit to eat!

We gived it to the dog. He liked it.

I asked my dad if'n them swamp rabbits was any good to eat.

He sed, "No. They taste like mud. I guess it's what they eat."

The day had been a long day. Guess if'n we didn't have nothang else to eat we coulda et it. But I knowed my mama'd have somethang good to eat.

She shore were a good cook. They all worked hard and had very little to show for it. But they taught us to work hard and to never hurt nobody.

Years later I were in North Korea and we runned out of food. At that point I thank I'd a et that green possum.
Red Fussell

Deer Huntin'

Chapter 57

My dad asked me if'n I'd like to go deer huntin'.

I sed, "I shore would."

So he got me a permit. It were real cold in the Ocala Forest. We spent the night in a tarpaper shack. They had a wood stove inside, so I went over to the swamp afore we left to git my sleepin' bag. My dad got a bag of food.

We went with preacher Goodwin. My dad hunted with 'im ever' year.

We left Okahumpka and picked Rev. Goodwin up in Leesburg. We went through Weirsdale, 'cross the Ocala River and turned at the South Tower. It were still dark when we got there, but they had a big fire built. It shore felt good.

I taked my .20 guage with some buckshot shells. My dad gived me 2 Black Cow candy bars. He sed, "I'm gonna put y'all on a deer stand. The deer have horns and if'n it has a spike it'll be 'bout 5 inches long."

He told me to not make no noise and not to move. I heered the dog runnin' a deer. They went to my right, but I didn't see nothang. Then I looked and a deer were easin' through the brush. He stuck 'is head up. It had horns. I raised the gun and fired. I shot 'im in the side

169

of the head. He jumped in the air and then fell.

My dad come up fast and wanted to know what I shot. We walked out where the deer layed. It were a nice size deer.

We gutted it out so it would cool quick. We got back in the truck and a man come up to the truck and sed, "My dog was runnin' that deer, so I should git half of that-there deer."

The game warden come up 'bout that time. It were Ed.

The one that tried to catch us in the swamp were the same man that wanted half of our deer.

Ed sed, "Them dogs are at the breedin' ground. They was chasin' that deer., Y'all done this afore. I know who y'all are."

Then Ed asked 'im for 'is huntin' license. He didn't have none. So Ed put 'im in the back of 'is car. He sed he were takin' 'im to jail.

I hadda tag my deer and check 'im at the checkin' station. After we done that we left for home. I shore woulda liked to camp, but we was goin' home.

We got home and put the deer skin on the side of the barn to dry out. My dad cut the back strap and my mama cooked it. And she made some biskets and sweet taters and put some ham in it that were smoked. Then she cut some ribs and mixed 'em with pork and fried it like hamburger. He cut the horns off and nailed 'em on the barn.

Rev. Goodwin had never kilt a deer. He were a good man and a good hunter.

He told me, "Y'all may never kill 'nother deer, but it were fun to hunt them."

Then he told me, "Y'all can't go back and hunt 'cause y'all can only kill one deer a season.

I asked 'im, "Can I jist go to the woods?"

He sed, "Shore."

The next week my dad kilt a big deer. So, that ended our huntin' for the year.

It were over 15 years afore I kilt 'nother deer.
Red Fussell

Skeeters and Hogs and Mules, Oh My!

Florida Deer   *Peg Urban*

War Bonds

Chapter 58

We caught a ride to Leesburg. We wanted to see an Army tank. If'n y'all bought a war bond y'all could look inside. I shore wanted to do that. We didn't have no shoes on. I guess we shoulda wore shoes, but they hurt our feet.

When we got there they jist looked at us like we was white trash. I didn't care that they sold stamps. They was 10 cents, so we didn't buy none. We walked by the tank. The man settin' on it were in the Army.

He sed, "Boys, would y'all like to see inside?"

Sed, "We shore would."

We climbed on the tank. Then he let us go inside. We was happy as we could be. They were a bunch of stuff in the tank. I'd really like to go for a ride. Maybe some day I would.

We walked out to Hwy 27 and sticked out our thumbs. A man picked us up in a cattle truck. It smelled real bad, but it beat walkin'. We told 'im we went to see a tank and they let us inside.

We got out at Okahumpka. He were goin' on to Center Hill. Then we walked to Byron's house. He got 'is .22 mag rifle. We walked over to Stage Coach Road and on to Cason Hammock.

They warn't much goin' on there, so we went to Bugg Spring Run.

Skeeters and Hogs and Mules, Oh My!

They was some brim swimmin' 'round the grass, but that's all.

We started over to the swamp and hid 'cause they was 2 men with guns. I guess they was huntin' somethang to eat. Well, it musta been slim pickin'. They didn't have nothang.

We let 'em pass. We didn't know who they was.

Then we eased through the grove, walked in on the log and climbed in our tree house. Byron's sleeping bag were there. I'd brought my sleepin' bag back over, so we rolled 'em both out and laid on 'em. They shore felt good.

We wondered what happened to that man and 'is wife that sunk they's air boat. We 'membered how cold and wet they both was when they climbed up in our tree house with us.

We'd been there for 'bout an hour and didn't see one thang. Even the birds wasn't makin' no noise. So we thought we might as well go home.

We climbed down after we rolled our sleepin' bags up and left. We stopped at the hog pen. They's nobody swingin' even.

I told Byron, "I'm gonna go home."

My dad and mama always go to Leesburg on Saturday, so I were purty shore they was gone. I went out to our hog pen and rubbed the ole sow. I like to hear 'im moan and grunt.

Then I seen my dad come home. They'd been to the A&P Store.

It were jist a good day.

WW II Sherman Tank

173

Fish Fry

Chapter 59

The church wanted to have a fish fry. I telled Byron, "We could catch most of the fish."

He sed, "If'n we git caught in Shaw Pond, Sy might kill us! The pond is on 'is property."

Well, I knowed Sy don't like us, but I were shore willin' to try.

So Saturday mornin' we left Byron's house with our rods and reels. I had a John Dillin'. It were a sinker. Byron sed he used a Dalton Special.

We got us a piece of bailin' wire. We didn't walk down Clay Road this time. Instead, we went through the woods so nobody could see our footprints, and we didn't wear white clothes, neither. We put a feed sack over our heads, so we could hide.

I telled Byron, "Sy don't work on Saturday so we need to be on our guard."

We crossed the road, brushed out our foot prints, climbed through the fence and they were a posted sign jist 'bout ever' fencepost to keep out. I looked to see if'n they had our names on 'em.

My brother told me, "Someday they's gonna put y'all in jail!" He may be right, but I'd git out some day.

We waded out in the pond. It were jist full of fish, and we caught a

Skeeters and Hogs and Mules,
Oh My!

bunch of bass. I shook Byron, 'cause I seen Sy comin' on 'is horse. I jist knowed we was caught.

But we waded in the grass, pulled a bonnet and jist left our heads stickin' out enough to breathe. He rode by the pond. Then he rode 'round it twice. I jist knowed he seen us, but then he left.

We stayed hid for a little while. Then we seen 'im go through the woods. And we seen 'im go through the gate. I shore hoped he'd leave so we could git out.

Sy headed toward Mr. Hall's store. So I told Byron, "I thank we should go."

So we slipped through the woods and crossed the fence. We was 'cross the road when we seen 'im comin' back with the law.

I told Byron, "We need to go to the swamp real quick."

So we eased through the trees. We was in the clear and headed through to the pond in back of Byron's house. We made it.

We cleaned the bass and had a big ole pan full. Byron's dad had been fishin' with Clyde. They hadn't caught much, but we cleaned they's fish that they did catch. We had 'nough fish to cook Sunday after church.

Mr. Works told us somebody kilt a cow in the pasture and skinned it. They knowed who done it and were goin' there to put 'em in jail.

I told Byron, "I'm shore glad we didn't do that!"

In 'bout 2 weeks they put a man we didn't even know in jail. They sed he'd been in jail quite a bit.

We had the fish fry. Byron and me done the cookin'. We seen Sy go by. I thought, *I'll bet he'd like to have some of this fish.*

Mr. Works stopped Sy and gived 'im a plate. He laffed and sed, "These fish eat like the fish in the Shaw Pond."

We jist looked at 'im.

We fished the Shaw Pond many many times!
Red Fussell

James Carlton Fussell

Pond Bonnets   *Peg Urban*

The Creek

Chapter 60

It were a sunny day and kinda hot. So we decided to go to the creek and take a swim. Betty Jean wanted to go with us, and then Melba wanted to go. By the time we got to the creek we had a whole crowd. Along the way we picked up Catfish, RH and Paul.

We all walked over to the creek. We was gonna pull some grass to float on. The creek were full so we had to watch for snakes.

We got down in the creek and started to pull some grass. Then I told ever'one to git out of the creek real quick. They wanted to know why they hada git out.

I told 'em, "They's a big gator in the grass."

He were lookin' for one of us. All y'all could see were 'is eye. I told Bryon, "He's gotta be at least 10 feet long."

Byron sed, "We should kill 'im".

I told 'im, "We could make some money off 'im."

The rest of the bunch stayed there while Byron and me went to Byron's house. We hooked up Charley, got our gator hook, stopped by the house and got a piece of hog belly and put a small boat in the wagon. Then we got the .22 mag, so we thought we had ever'thang we needed.

When we got back, the gator done moved. The other kids showed us where he'd went. So Byron paddled the boat close to where he were and throwed the hog belly with a big hook in it close to 'im.

The gator grabbed it. So Byron paddled the boat back. The gator were on the line.

We took Charley loose. We was gonna pull that-there gator out of the creek. We didn't ask Charley if'n he wanted to do it, we jist done it.

I snatched on the rope to set the hook. We had 'im. He were rollin' and tryin' to git loose, but he were hooked. We tied the rope to Charley's trace chain and Byron told 'im to "git up."

I got the .22 mag, but made shore they were a shell in it first.

That ole gator didn't like what we was doin'. He were rollin' and tryin' to git loose. We had 'im comin' to the edge of the creek.

All them on the bank run. I wished I had too. When the gator come on the bank he run.

Charley seen the gator and he run. Byron fell down and the gator went by Byron. Him and Charley was movin' on.

I run tryin' to catch Charley. The gator got on the side of a tree and stopped Charley. I run up and shot the gator. He died real quick.

Byron unhooked Charley from the rope and Charley took off with Byron holdin' on. Finally, Charley stopped, and we got 'im back.

We skinned the gator, cut 'is tail off and split the belly and pushed it in the creek.

Charley didn't even like the hide in the wagon. So we hid the hide under the wagon.

I telled Byron, "Let's take the meat to Mr. Mike. He lives not far from where we is."

We all loaded up and rode down the creek to Mr. Mike's house.

When we got there 'is son were there. He still smelt like a pole cat. That stuff shore stays with y'all. I bet he thanks comin' out to see a green possum jist warn't worth it. That pole cat got all of 'em real good.

We asked 'im if'n he'd seen any green possums lately. He didn't thank that were funny.

We gived 'im the gator meat and he got all of us a soda water. We thanked 'im and telled 'im we hada go home.

We went back home on the highway. Ed, the game warden, come

Skeeters and Hogs and Mules, Oh My!

by; but he jist waved at us.

I told Byron, "He woulda put us in jail if'n he knowed what we done."

We dropped me by my house with my .22 mag. When I walked in the house my brother wanted to know what I'd skinned.

I told 'im, "A big gator."

Then my mama walked in and told me to go take a bath. She thought I didn't smell very good. I really don't like to take a bath in the middle of the week, but I don't like sleepin' in the barn neither.

Byron and me killed lots of big gators.
Red Fussell

Florida Gator

The Drum

Chapter 61

A man gived me a big ole 55-gallon drum. My dad told me we could cut the top out and clean hogs in it.

So I rolled it down to Mr. Earl's Repair Shop. He worked on cars all the time. He shore were a nice person. I asked Mr. Earl how to cut the top out of the drum.

He smelled it and told me I needed to flash it. So I asked 'im how to do that.

He sed, "Get a fat liter splinter. Put it in front of the openin.'"

I rolled the drum back home and put it by a big oak tree. I put it on one side and I got on the other side. I lit the splinter and reached 'round the tree. When the fire went by the drum it made a real big noise. It shook people's houses and my ears hummed for a few days.

When I looked on the other side, both ends had blowed out. It done blowed the drum up!

I taked all the pieces to show Mr. Earl what happened, but they warn't much there.

He jist laffed. He told me I shoulda filled the drum with water.

Well, it were too late now.

Now it wouldn't even hold no water.

Ducks

Chapter 62

We was at Mr. Hall's store. They were a man talkin' 'bout all the ducks on Clear Water Lake.

So I asked Byron if'n he wanted to go duck huntin'.

He didn't wanna go. He were goin' with 'is dad to Terry Town for somethang.

So I walked home, got my .20 gauge shotgun and walked over to Clear Water Lake. I walked all 'round the edge of the lake. I didn't see no ducks at all.

I went by the island and there I seen movement in the water. So I laid in the grass. Out swimmed 'bout 8 ducks. They was feedin'. Some was up and some was down.

I crawled to the edge of the lake and then I looked a big ole snake right in the eye! Guess he were more 'fraid of me and he crawled off real quick.

Them ducks hadn't seen me. I crawled as quiet as I could, and got 3 shells in my hand. Then 4 ducks come up. I shore hoped they'd git in a line 'cause then I could hit the front one and kill all 4 of 'em.

I loaded the gun and shot the first one. Then 4 of 'em was kilt. I loaded 'gain real quick and kilt 2 more.

I shucked my clothes to keep 'em dry. Then I waded out to git the ducks. I wrung the neck on the one floppin'.

I headed to the bank carryin' the ducks and knowed I were in big trouble. They were a gator between me and the bank. I guess he smelt the blood from the duck. I'd walk one way, and and he'd swim with me. If'n I stopped, he stopped. My shotgun were layin' on the bank. I knowed I made a big mistake and I knowed I couldn't out-run 'im in the water.

The only thang I could do were to throw 'im a duck. So I throwed it far 'nough to git out of the water. He grabbed the duck and swallowed it.

By that time I were on the bank and loaded the gun. He'd out-run me if'n I run. So I stayed my ground and then throwed 'im 'nother duck on the bank.

He come after it and I shot 'im on the back of 'is head. It kilt 'im.

Boy! I were a-shakin'. I'd made a big mistake, but I got out of it.

If'n that gator hadn't got greedy, he'd still be alive.

I looked at 'im layin' on the ground. I taked my knife and skinned the hide off 'im. I cut the belly open and got my duck back.

Now, I still were in trouble. I'd have the gator meat and the ducks to carry home. So I tied the ducks' feet with my belt and put that 'round my neck. I didn't have a duck stamp to legally hunt ducks. And I had a gator hide which were also illegal. So if'n I got caught, I never would git out of jail.

I made a sling for my gun. I were 'bout 2 miles from home. I were carryin' more weight than I weighed. I couldn't walk down the road, which would be the shortest way. I'd have to go through the woods. I knowed it were gonna be tuff.

I started walkin' and then I heered a truck start up. I jist knowed it were Ed, the game warden. So I hid in the bushes.

But up drove the snake man. I asked 'im if'n he'd take me home.

He sed, "Shore."

And he taked me right to my front door.

So I asked if'n he'd like 2 ducks first.

He sed, "No." But I gived 'im 2 ducks anyway.

I taked my gator meat and the other ducks in the back of the house.

Skeeters and Hogs and Mules, Oh My!

We cut the gator meat in strips and hung 'em to dry. My mama soaked some of the strips in honey and salted 'em down. We put the gator meat in the smoke house. They was already smokin' some ham out there.

My mama built a fire 'round the big ole wash pot. When we had the gator all done, the water in the wash pot was hot. So we dipped the ducks in the hot water. It made the feathers come off real easy.

Then when we picked off most of 'em feathers and my mama singed the ducks. I opened 'em ducks up and got the livers and the gizzards out and cleaned 'em. My mama went inside and fired up the wood stove. She fried the livers and gizzards and baked all the ducks. It takes longer to bake the ducks than to fry 'em.

My dad come home 'bout then and seen what we was doin'. He checked the gator to make shore we done it right. He dipped 'em strips in honey and then told me they was gonna be tuff. I shoulda boiled the meat first, but we'd eat it anyway.

Then he wanted to know where I kilt 'em.

I told 'im, "By the island."

Then I told 'im 'bout the gator.

He told me he'd done the same thang once and sed, "Bet y'all don't lay y'all's gun down 'gain!"

Then my dad told me to be careful 'cause Ed, the game warden were all over Okahumpka.

I got a man to sell my gator hide and got 9 dollars for it. So I bought shells for my gun with the money.

I told my dad I gived the snake man 2 ducks for bringin' me home.

I kilt lots of ducks on Clear Water Lake, but
this were the time I nearly didn't live to take 'em home.
Red Fussell

James Carlton Fussell

Duck Stamp (hunting license)

Hooded Mergansers   *Peg Urban*

The Trip to Clear Water Lake

Chapter 63

I told Byron 'bout the ducks on Clear Water Lake, so we hitched up Charley and got our shotguns. We was gonna kill some more ducks.

We worked the edge of the lake. When we come to where I shot the gator, he were rotten and the buzzards done picked 'im clean. We knocked 'is teeth out. We could use 'em to make us some necklaces like our rattle snake necklaces.

They jist warn't no ducks on the lake that day. We come round the corner and guess who were standin' there. Mr. Ed, the game warden. He wanted to know what we was huntin'. We told 'im rattlesnakes. We wanted to git they's skins.

Ed sed, "Y'all boys kill that gator?"

Byron sed, "No, I didn't do it."

I jist didn't say nothin'.

Then he sed, "Did Bill kill 'im?"

Byron sed, "I don't know."

We told Mr. Ed we was gonna shoot snipes. They's hard to hit.

So he told us, "They's a bunch of 'em jist 'round that bend."

We tied Charley to the tree. Ed were right.

When we spooked a snipe Byron kilt 'im.

I seen a duck fly in and telled Byron, "I'd like to shoot that duck, but Mr. Ed would put us in jail."

Then somebody shot somewhere and we seen Mr. Ed goin' through the woods. We kilt 3 snipes in 'bout an hour.

We looked up and here come Mr. Ed with Bill. He had Bill's gun and 2 ducks.

I asked Mr. Ed, "Could I have the ducks?"

He sed, "No, them ducks is evidence. I have to take 'em to court."

We left and went by Mr. Mike settin' on the porch. We asked 'im if'n he'd like to have some snipe.

He sed he'd never ate no snipe and asked, "Is it white meat? Is it bigger than a quail?"

We sed. "They's good."

We cleaned 'em and saved the liver and heart and gizzard and gived 'em to 'im too.

Mrs. Sweetie Pie sed she'd cook 'em.

We got on the wagon and started home. We come by the school and Mr. Ed stopped us.

He sed, "What'd y'all boys kill?"

We telled 'im, "Jist 3 snipes, and we give 'em to Mr. Mike."

Mr. Ed sed, "I know y'all boys would kill jist what y'all sed. Jist leave some for seed."

It'd been like a game. I hope we never loose. It's a job to 'im and a game to us.

We never got caught, but we should have.
Red Fussell

Snipe

Skeeters and Hogs and Mules, Oh My!

The Spring

Chapter 64

We decided to go to Bugg Spring. Joe lived down there and he had 'lectric trains. Sometimes he'd let us play with 'em.

I guess Joe's house were the only house in Okahumpka that had 'lectricity. I'd never even seen a 'lectric stove, but Joe's mama turned 'ers on. I put my hand right on it and it burnt a perfect ring on my hand. I still have the scar today.

I told Byron, after I burnt it, that I hada go home. When I got home my mama had a plant she put on the burn. It were sore for a few days and blistered up. And then it were all right.

Joe come to the Okahumpka school too. We teached 'im how to fly a horsefly. First y'all gotta catch the horsefly. Then y'all tie a sewin' thread to 'is leg and turn 'im loose, but y'all hold the other end of the thread. He'd fly 'round and 'round.

We went back to the spring. Joe's mama taked us to Leesburg in the boat. They's boat had a motor on the back. We shore couldn't paddle that fast! It didn't take long and we come back jist as fast.

When we got back, we went swimmin' in the spring. That-there spring is 170 feet deep. They's a tree that's got a big limb we used to jump off into the spring. The spring were 'bout 30 feet deep right there.

James Carlton Fussell

Not ever'body would jump. Byron would and I would, but my brother wouldn't. He couldn't swim.

We was walkin' the edge of the spring and seen a big gator come close to the bank. Joe eased up to the gator and jumped on 'is back. He rode 'im a short way, but sed it were a rough ride.

I never did try that, 'cause gators like to eat ever'thang they see.

They was a bamboo patch we played in, but the bamboo had a fuzz that made us itch. I hada take 2 baths to git rid of the itch.

Ever'body swimmed in the spring. The water were clean and y'all could see the fish, but they wouldn't bite.

Joe still lives on Bugg Spring
Red Fussell

Horsefly

Skeeters and Hogs and Mules, Oh My!

Charley

Chapter 65

I were out back feedin' the hogs. Byron come and told me that Charley were gone and he didn't know where he were.

So I told my mama I were gonna go over to Byron's 'cause Charley were missin'. He'd never walked off afore. I shore hope nobody stoled 'im.

The fence were down on the back side of the hog pen, but Charley never tried to leave. He always had plenty of food, and we shore didn't beat 'im. He were the best ole mule. He'd never tried to bite us or kick us.

We walked to the hog pen. He warn't there. We looked all over the pasture. He warn't there. We walked by the pond back of Byron house. They warn't no tracks.

We went to where the fence were down. They were 'is tracks. He'd gone through the woods. We looked to see if'n someday led 'im out, but only Charley's tracks was there. He were goin' to Lake Dunham Swamp.

When we got to the grove, we found 'is tracks and follered 'im through the grove. Ever' once in a while he'd lay down. I didn't know what to thank 'bout that.

We was still trackin' 'im. He didn't seem to be in no hurry. We were almost to where our treehouse were. And there we seen Charley. He were layin' on the ground.

We walked up and I told Byron, "He's dead. He ain't breathin'."

We felt 'im. He were cold.

I told Byron, "He were lookin' for us."

And I cried, "Why did he have to die?"

We shore had lots of fun with 'im. He didn't git in no hurry, but we didn't care.

We went back and told Byron's dad 'bout Charley. He he come down with 'is truck and loaded 'im on the back.

We hauled 'im to the hog pen. Then 'bout ever'body helped us dig a hole to put 'im in. We covered 'im up.

I told Byron, "Let's plant a big tall tree over 'im."

We made a tombstone and wrote 'is name on it. And we wrote our names on 'is tombstone too. We wrote, "We Love You Charley."

The next day at Mr. Hall's store, Miss Sweetie Pie asked if'n we'd mow 'er grass.

We told 'er we couldn't 'cause Charley died.

She told us she'd buy us a new mule. But we told 'er, "We can't replace Charley."

As I write this-here book, I jist can't go on. This is where the book stops. I don't know if'n I'll ever write 'nother book.

"Bye Charley."

Red Fussell

Skeeters and Hogs and Mules, Oh My!

James Carlton Fussell

PICTURE ALBUM

Floyd Jagger family. Red went to school with the little girl.

Train boxcars behind these men were used to ship
watermelons from Okahumpka.

Skeeters and Hogs and Mules,
Oh My!

All Jagger children, except for Evelyn (third back).
She is 91 this year, 2017

This child is probably Red.

Skeeters and Hogs and Mules,
Oh My!

Lydon (left) and Dale, Red's long-time friends.
He's known Lydon since high sschool days.

James Carlton Fussell

Ronald, Woody, Wilbur, Red

Skeeters and Hogs and Mules, Oh My!

POEMS

Mule
There was a mule named Charley.
We bought him for a dollar.
Everytime we looked at him
He'd holler. He warn't no scholar.
But he liked to holler.
I think we wasted our dollar!
Red Fussell

Well
I looked in the well
It looks like me
What did I see?
It must be me.

The water was deep, but not asleep.
It was a lot like me
I dropped a rock in the well and it splashed
It still looks like me
It was there for me to see.
Red Fussell

Man
There was a man, mean as he could be
Had five kids, I'm glad it wasn't me.
When he whipped one, he whipped three.
Most would hide in the tree. I'm glad it wasn't me.
He looked up in the tree and saw three.
And then he whipped me!
Red Fussell

James Carlton Fussell

Epilogue

My name is Red Fussell. I've lived in Okahumpa all my life, except 2 years when Uncle Sam sent me a draft notice that my friend and neighbor wanted me to go in the Army for 2 years. I never did find out who my friend and neighbor was. But I seen Korea and the world.

I wrote my first book at age 83 and titled it *Tall Sawgrass* for a very close friend, Byron. He were dying. We went to press jist one week afore he passed away. But I was able to read most of the chapters to 'im as we went along.

Thank You

This book woulda never happened without the help of these two ladies, Sandy Kruse and Ruth Williams. Thank you, Sandy and Ruth.